How to Get an A Grade

Effective learning involves reducing difficult topics into smaller, "bite-sized" chunks.

Every revision guide, card or coursebook from PushMe Press comes with its own website consisting of summaries, handouts, games, model essays, revision notes and more. Each website community is supported by the best teachers in the country.

At the end of each chapter you will see an `i-pu-sh` web link that you can type into your web browser along with a QR code that can be scanned by our free app.

These links will give you immediate access to the additional resources you need to "Get an A Grade" by providing you with the relevant information needed.

Getting an A Grade has never been easier.

Download our FREE How to Get an A Grade in Philosophy App for your phone or tablet and get up-to-date information that accompanies this book and the whole PushMe Press range.

D1322399

http://philosophy.pushmepress.com/download

Ontological Argument & the Relationship Between Reason & Faith

Key terms

- **ANALYTIC STATEMENT** - A statement where the predicate is contained within the subject, eg "married men are husbands", or, for Anselm, "God [subject] necessarily exists [predicate]".

- **A POSTERIORI** - Knowledge gained after experience.

- **A PRIORI** - Knowledge gained prior to experience.

- **CONTINGENT EXISTENCE** - Something which, by its nature, does not necessarily have to exist, and could or could not have existence, eg you or me. Once existent, can go out of existence.

- **DEDUCTION** - A type of reasoning whereby it is demonstrated that the conclusion necessarily follows from the premises (as seen in the ontological argument).

- **IMMUTABLE** - Not capable of or susceptible to change; unalterable.

Please support our learning community by not photocopying without a licence

- **INDUCTION** - A type of reasoning that takes specific instances and from them draws a general conclusion (eg as seen in the cosmological argument).

- **NECESSARY BEING** - A being whose non-existence is a contradiction.

- **ONTOLOGICAL** - Words or wisdom (logos) about being (ontos). What it means for something to be.

- **PREDICATE** - A property of a subject, for example tall, round; for Anselm, necessary existence is a predicate of the greatest possible being.

- **REDUCTIO AD ABSURDUM** - An argument that shows that the opposite of what it is claiming cannot be true.

- **SYNTHETIC STATEMENT** - A statement where the predicate is not contained with the subject, eg "married men are happy", and some knowledge of the world is required to assess its validity.

The ontological argument (OA) for the existence of God (a title **KANT** gave to this argument) is the only argument studied that does not start from empirical evidence and work back to God (the latter types of arguments are **A POSTERIORI** and inductive in nature). The OA commences with a definition of God given by **ANSELM** which, once understood, entails actual (and then in a later argument) **NECESSARY** existence.

ANSELM'S ONTOLOGICAL ARGUMENT

The first form of the argument is found in the Proslogion (Discourse on the Existence of God), chapter 2:

- God is the greatest possible being that can be thought of.

- If God exists only in the mind (or understanding), then a greater being could be conceived to exist both in the mind and in reality.

- This "greatest possible being" (of premise one) must therefore exist in the mind and in reality.

Therefore God must exist as a being in reality (in re) as well as in the mind (in intellectu).

Anselm was writing with reference to **PSALMS 14** and **53** where it notes that "the fool says in his heart there is no God". He stated that the fool understood that God is "that than which nothing greater can be conceived".

Anselm argued that the fool, once he understood this, logically had to acknowledge that it was not possible for such a being to exist in thought alone, as then there would be a greater being who existed in thought and reality.

Anselm noted that it would be **CONTRADICTORY** to state, once the fool has in his mind the greatest possible being, that such a being cannot exist, as existence in reality is an intrinsic quality in the greatest being (by definition). Therefore God exists.

Chapter 3 of the Proslogion developed this argument by stating again that God is the greatest possible being, and that, as such, has

NECESSARY EXISTENCE. God cannot not be, and a necessary state of being is always greater than **CONTINGENT EXISTENCE**, which is dependent on other things for existence (again, think you or me). If the state of necessary existence is greater than contingent existence, and God is the greatest possible being, God must be, uniquely, a **NECESSARY** being, entirely not dependent on anything else for existence, ie intrinsically necessary.

Something having the possibility of not existing or coming in and going out of existence - a **CONTINGENT** being - will always be less than that which cannot not exist. Anselm's claim was that the predicate of existence is an intrinsic part of the concept of God just as a spinster has the predicate of "being unmarried" (this will be important later when **KANT** critiques Anselm), and this type of argument, where the **PREDICATE** (exists necessarily) is contained in the **SUBJECT** (God) is known as an **ANALYTIC STATEMENT**. The idea of God not existing is a logical impossibility and hence Anselm's argument is a **REDUCTIO AD ABSURDUM**. Remember that this is an argument based on the consideration of the very "beingness" or intrinsic nature of God, not on a posteriori evidence from the world that may lead us to conclude there is a God.

GAUNILO'S CHALLENGE TO ANSELM'S ARGUMENT AND ANSELM'S REPLY

GAUNILO, a French monk and contemporary to Anselm, wrote On Behalf of the Fool as a response to Anselm. He argued that someone could imagine something like a beautiful island, and think that this was the most excellent, **PERFECT** island. Using Anselm's reasoning, Gaunilo argued that for the island to really be the greatest island it must exist in reality as well as in the imagination. If it did not exist in reality it would not be the greatest island. You can apply Gaunilo's point here to anything and say because it is perfect it must exist in reality, not just in the mind.

Gaunilo said that this island obviously does not exist just because we have imagined it to be so, defined it as the greatest and then said that because it is the greatest that means it must have existence. Gaunilo suggested that those who believe such an island existed because of this reasoning are either joking or foolish, and anyone who believed them would likewise be a **FOOL**. He used this counter-example to challenge Anselm on his argument for God's existence which, as outlined above, goes along similar lines and, Gaunilo suggests, is as flawed as the argument for the island's existence.

We cannot just define things into existence.

ANSELM'S REPLY TO GAUNILO

Gaunilo's criticism concentrates on the first formulation of **ANSELM'S** argument about things existing in the mind and reality. In Anselm's Reply to Gaunilo he emphasised that the island he used in his example is **CONTINGENT**, and would never have to exist in the way that God as a necessary being has to, as the greatest thing that can be thought. It is logically conceivable to think that the island could not exist, unlike God.

God as the greatest thing that can be thought is, by his very nature, in a category of one, and is something that cannot not exist or be greater or bettered.

The island however could always have one more palm tree, or a bluer sea, and could either not exist, or exist without perfection, as that is not something of its intrinsic nature. **PLANTINGA** noted that, unlike the greatest being that can be thought of, God, islands have no **INTRINSIC** maximum. A contingent island and a necessary God cannot be compared.

DESCARTES' ONTOLOGICAL ARGUMENT

In Meditation 5 of Meditations on Philosophy, Descartes built on his previous thought that certain truths are, by their very nature, impossible to be doubted, and that people are innately able to understand that some things cannot be different, ie, equality and shape. He thought that one **INNATE IDEA** people had was a concept of God as a perfect being.

Working from this and drawing on his background as a mathematician, Descartes argued that there are certain things that have an unchangeable nature, and we know that this is the case. He used the example of a triangle. Essential to its nature are "three angles equal to two right angles", and the nature of the triangle could not be different; it is **IMMUTABLE**.

God's nature is likewise immutable, and part of that **IMMUTABLE NATURE** is having all perfections, of which one is existence. Triangles have essential characteristics, without which they would not be triangles; God has the essential characteristic of existence, without which such a being could not be God.

However, what if it could be argued that we can think of a triangle which has to have certain characteristics for it to be a triangle, but then acknowledge that such a triangle doesn't have to exist in reality? **DESCARTES** noted this but said that existence is a perfection, and as God, by definition and as part of his essence, has all perfections, he has to exist in a way that a triangle has to have internal angles of 180 degrees.

It is a contradiction to claim otherwise, but it is simply that the triangle doesn't have existence as one of its necessary essences, whereas God does.

(Note here that Descartes is claiming that existence is "more perfect" than non-existence, as Anselm said existence was part of the greatest being). An object has to have certain **NECESSARY** things for it to be that object; it cannot be separated from those characteristics. Descartes used a further example of a mountain which cannot exist without a valley; likewise, it is not possible to talk of God (and God alone, not any contingent items) without perfection, and existence is a **PERFECTION**.

KANT'S OBJECTIONS

Kant argued that existence is not a **PREDICATE** like green or tall. The latter help to describe the object. "Existence" cannot be used in that way, as existence refers to the whole object.

All that Descartes has done is to say, "if a triangle exists it has interior angles adding up to 180 degrees"; similarly Kant argued that the **ONTOLOGICAL ARGUMENT** says, if God exists he is a necessary being, but this does not mean he does exist in reality.

Kant argued that "existence is not a predicate". A **PREDICATE** is something that adds to our knowledge of what a subject is like, for example, such a thing is big or brown or flat. **EXISTENCE** doesn't work in this way, as it does not tell us anything about the object that helps us in the identification of that object. Existence is actually the thing and all its characteristics, rather than just another predicate.

For example, if I say that my boat is fast, I give more information about the boat, but if I say the boat exists then I add nothing to the description of it; I am actually saying that there is a real example of this boat, and this is not what the role of a predicate is. Try this in reverse: If I say, "the boat does not exist" then I have not actually just taken away one property (or predicate) of the boat but have taken away the entire boat.

What **KANT** noted was that when we say something exists we are saying that such an object has been **ACTUALISED**, but he argued that we cannot simply add existence to the concept of God and say we have proved or actualised the existence of such a concept. Noting the essential characteristics of a triangle as certain angles only actually gets us as far as saying, "IF a triangle existed it would have these characteristics".

Believing that God exists, and, following on from that belief to say that God has necessary existence, is not an argument that God necessarily has to exist in reality, just like triangles do not have to have existence, although if they did they would have certain predicates.

If there is a God, he has necessary existence, but the predicate of necessary existence cannot be declared as intrinsic to God and a claim made that as a consequence God has to exist in reality.

Kant thus argues that it is not contradictory to think of a possible being who has **NECESSARY** existence. To describe something as having characteristics would give us a picture of something if it existed, but by describing something, even by saying something has necessary existence, does not establish the existence of that thing. For Kant, all statements about existence are **SYNTHETIC**, true or false after verification, and not analytic, meaning "true by nature". The existence of God needs to be verified from a position exterior to the concept as it were, not by **ANALYTIC** analysis of the term.

If **ANSELM** and **DESCARTES** think they have overcome this idea by suggesting that God has necessary existence as one of the characteristics of the greatest or perfect being, and only this predicate can be assigned to God, then they are in danger of making a circular argument. Are they suggesting that God exists necessarily on the grounds that God has necessary existence?

Has Descartes convinced you that necessary existence has to entail actual existence? Or, as **CATERUS** argued, is this not enough and Descartes still has to show that the "concept of necessary existence entails actual existence" (in Lacewing)?

A modern day reply to Kant has come from **NORMAN MALCOLM**.

After outlining the idea of an unlimited being as one that does not depend on anything for its existence (meaning God is not contingent), and also that if God does not exist then he cannot come into existence, Malcolm put forward the following formulation:

- The existence of an unlimited being is either logically impossible or logically necessary.

- God's existence is not logically impossible, as there is no logical contradiction in the concept of a God/unlimited being who exists (the idea is not logically absurd or internally contradictory).

- God's existence is therefore logically necessary.

But again, has Malcolm answered the key problem of whether the concept of God as necessary entails existence in reality? Does it mean that if the existence of God is not impossible, it is **NECESSARY**, or just **POSSIBLE**? (It is worth reading the Malcolm extract at the end of the chapter.)

Scholars have noted that Malcolm may have proved the concept of the **LOGICAL NECESSITY** of God's existence (that the non-existence of God is a logical impossibility and self-contradictory), but not the existence of God in reality or factually.

Words and concepts do not always describe realities, even when those concepts have internal and logical consistency.

Strengths

- There is some attraction to a **DEDUCTIVE** and **ANALYTIC** argument that appeals to logical consistency rather than the mixed evidence for God from a posteriori evidence. It is an argument that has received much attention due to the fact that there does seem something to be wrong with it, but what that something is is not always apparent.

- Anselm and Descartes both responded to criticism that was levelled at their versions of the OA, and stressed what it means for God to be the **GREATEST POSSIBLE BEING** and necessary by definition. Examples of the greatest or perfect contingent things might therefore not count against what Anselm and Descartes argued. Some have argued that with Malcolm's reformulation of the OA, the argument still holds importance.

- Does Kant's critique of Descartes' OA hold? It might be that saying that "something exists", for example, Spiderman, does add something new to the description because up until that point the listener would have been thinking of a fictional character. Jackson points out that the atheist may be thinking of God as a fictional character so the addition of "and exists" may actually change the definition of the word God, and thus existence, in that sense, may act as a predicate.

Weaknesses

- The Proslogion was written by a monk as a prayer - can it be used as an argument for the existence of God? Rather, is it a support to those who already believe? Is it, more properly, **FAITH SEEKING UNDERSTANDING**?

- Is existence in reality **NECESSARILY** and in all cases greater than existence in the mind only? This is a value judgement. Are there counter-examples to this, with even one counter-example being enough to throw doubt on Anselm's position? The many wonderful qualities you imagine when you think of a future partner may never actually be found to be the case in reality, where you might be disappointed.

- Many scholars hold that Kant has delivered a fatal blow to Descartes' OA, by his argument that going from the concept of God having **NECESSARY EXISTENCE** to God **EXISTING IN REALITY** is flawed and that existence cannot act as a predicate.

Issues arising

- Does the ontological argument have any value for the non-believer?

- Does it successfully challenge disbelief in God?

- How successful is the argument as proof of God's existence?

- Would the success or failure of this argument have any significance for faith?

Key quotes

1. *"I do not seek to understand that I believe, but I believe in order to understand."* Anselm

2. *"From the fact that I cannot think of God except as existing, it follows that existence is inseparable from God, and hence that he really exists."* Descartes

3. *"Descartes' argument is only convincing for the claim that if God exists, God exists necessarily."* Lacewing

4. *"It would be self-contradictory to posit a triangle and yet reject its three angles, but there is no contradiction in rejecting the triangle together with its three angles."* Kant

5. *"The ontological argument is 'a charming joke'."* Schopenhauer

6. *"If God, a being greater than that which cannot be conceived, does not exist, then He cannot come into existence. Assuming that this is not so, if follows that He must necessarily exist."* Malcolm

Confusions to avoid

- "Gaunilo is an atheist" - not so. He believed in God but did not think Anselm's argument about the greatest possible being existing in reality as well as in the mind worked.
- Be very careful to know the differences between Anselm's first and second formulations, and then the difference between what Anselm is arguing and what Descartes (and even Malcolm, though he is not on the syllabus) is putting forward in their different ontological arguments.
- This is a topic that calls for **PRECISE DEFINITIONS** and these are perfectly possible if you pay attention to the different arguments that are being put forward. Learn and use technical terms, such as **A PRIORI**, **DEDUCTIVE** and **ANALYTIC**, to demonstrate your knowledge of the argument, and then do put forward your response to the various scholars' views you have heard - you are expected to show personal and philosophical engagement with the arguments.

GET MORE HELP

Get more help with the ontological argument and the relationship between reason and faith by using the links below:

http://i-pu.sh/T9V35W32

Religious Language

Key terms

- **ANALOGY** - When two things are compared as similar because they share common features, eg "the brain is like a computer".

- **ANALYTIC STATEMENT** - The internal logic of the sentence gives it its meaning.

- **BLIK** - A way of looking at the world. (Hare)

- **COGNITIVE** - Language that carries meaning, and puts forward a proposition, provable true or false.

- **EQUIVOCAL** - Where the same word is used in two different and unrelated ways, eg someone is at the sink, and someone is starting to sink.

- **FALSIFICATION PRINCIPLE** - A statement is putting forward a genuine scientific proposition if there are conditions under which that proposition can be falsified.

- **LANGUAGE GAME** - Individual terms have meaning because of the way they are used within a group (Wittgenstein). A form of life is the activities that the group performs using this language.

Please support our learning community by not photocopying without a licence

- **MYTH** - A story which conveys a religious belief or truth.

- **NON-COGNITIVE** - Does not carry meaning in a factual manner, and is not putting forward a proposition provable true or false.

- **REALIST** - Claims that refer to something that objectively exists, not something that exists just within the community of believers (anti-realist).

- **STRONG VERIFICATION PRINCIPLE** - A statement carries meaning only if it is either analytic or empirically verifiable.

- **UNIVOCAL** - Where the same word is used in two different contexts but means the same thing: a black cat and a cat on the mat. The word cat has the one meaning in both sentences.

- **VIA NEGATIVA** (the Apophatic Way) - The way of talking about God by saying what He is not.

- **VIA POSITIVA** (the Cataphatic Way) - The way of talking about God by saying what He is.

- **WEAK VERIFICATION PRINCIPLE** - A statement carries meaning only if it is "either analytic or can be shown by experience to be probably true" (**BURNS** and **LAW**).

THE VIA NEGATIVA (VN)

The VN is also known as **THE APOPHATIC WAY**, taken from the Greek verb apophēmi, which means "to deny". The VN is an attempt to speak of God using **NEGATION** and stems from the mystical religious tradition, which emphasises the quest to find unity with God. However, God lies **BEYOND** ordinary perception and cannot be described in the same way in which we describe other objects: for example, this teapot is green or that sweatshirt is large. God cannot be described adequately using "the positive", because He is **INEFFABLE**; He defies expression or description.

When we attempt to use the affirmative and use words such as "powerful" about a strong person, we mean something completely different when we say God is powerful. This is called **EQUIVOCAL LANGUAGE**.

We can get some knowledge of God by the way of the negative - by saying what **GOD IS NOT** - and joining such "not" statements together to arrive at a closer idea of **WHAT GOD IS**. In this sense, language for the person who advocates the **VN** is not descriptive or containing knowledge (**COGNITIVE**), but, as Cole notes, is being used in a "functional and evocative" way.

For example, I could get directions to Fraser St by a series of negatives (don't turn right at the junction). **MAIMONIDES** (12th C), used the example of a ship; by about the time of the tenth negative answer to questions concerning what a ship is, the enquirer had almost arrived at an accurate idea of a ship.

The example of the man asking directions works when there are only three or four options. He knew where Fraser Street was because we have discounted every other option for him. But can we use this way for a description of God? No, but with a series of questions, and by joining the answers together, we should get closer to what God is via the negative.

The **VN** has a long history. You may recognise some Platonic tones, where there is an ultimate good beyond the cave world we inhabit, and of which we only see shadows. In the 3rd C **PLOTINUS**, a neo-Platonist (a movement which built on the work of Plato but also altered/adapted Platonism), argued that it was impossible to know the good as it is entirely separate from the world.

ST AUGUSTINE (4th C) and **DIONYSIUS** (also known as **PSEUDO-DIONYSIUS**, 6th C), both wrote about the use of the VN as part of the mystical tradition. Dionysius noted three stages, or "states of knowledge" (**JORDAN**) when talking about God"

1. **VIA NEGATIVA**

   States what God is not, because God is beyond all human categories of knowledge and being. He is "not" anything which we would try to describe such as "life" or "oneness" or "good". "There is no speaking of it, nor name, nor knowledge of it. Darkness and light, error and truth.[God] is none of these." (**HICK**) So God is beyond any positive assertion.

2. **STATE OF AFFIRMATION**

   Affirm what we know God is: we do know God has been revealed in the Bible as good and just. But these terms can only be taken symbolically.

3. **QUALIFICATION**

   When we say God is loving, He is utterly beyond loving as affirmed in the mystical tradition, which is always looking "beyond" descriptions which are limited by human language. Maimonides also argues that the **INEFFABILITY** of God cannot be expressed by positive assertions about God.

Strengths

- The **VN** avoids **ANTHROPOMORPHISM** (describing God in human terms). It can stop people getting the wrong idea about God as being "warrior-like", and taking this literally, as saying that God is some kind of divine warrior. The **VN** argues that God is entirely "not" like us.

- **LIMITATIONS OF LANGUAGE** as a vessel to adequately describe God. Reason, logic and arguments are blunt tools when it comes to the spiritual mystery that is God. **AHLUWALIA** points out that anything other than the idea that God is mystery makes God too small.

- **INEFFABILITY** - The **VN** goes beyond our everyday experience, and allows for recognition that God is not "over there" or, indeed, located anywhere, or "like this". God is entirely ineffable.

Weaknesses

- **CONTRADICTION** between God's ineffability and the revelation of the Bible of the physical person Jesus Christ. Dionysius may in fact have accepted Christ as "God revealed", ie a manifestation of God, but this is not "God hidden", who remains ineffable.

- **REALIST** affirmations made by believers seem to go further. God has certain positive characteristics, for example, a warrior or a mighty king. Within many of the world's religions, **TRUTH CLAIMS ARE NOT NEGATIVELY EXPRESSED**. Judaism,

Christianity and Islam believe that God has in fact revealed his nature and affirms that nature in their respective scriptures. Christian theologians argue that at the heart of the Christian faith is the affirmation that God is involved in the world, rather than beyond matter, life, humanity and any description.

- **DAVIES** does not think negatives can get us closer to the actual thing we are trying to describe.

- **BEGS THE QUESTION** - Every time we give a negative answer, we are showing that we already know what God is, and so the VN only works for those who already know who and what God is, which seems self-contradictory.

- **DEATH BY A THOUSAND QUALIFICATIONS** - By continually saying God is not this, and God is not that, **FLEW** contends that there is little difference between saying that "God is anything we can affirm" and "God does not exist" - "by saying that God is invisible, soundless, incorporeal and so on, there is very little difference between our definition of God and our definition of nothingness; we argue God out of existence by "a thousand qualifications". (**AHLUWALIA**)

Key quotes

1. *"We do not know what God is. God Himself does not know what He is because He is not anything. Literally God is not, because He transcends being."* Johannes Scotus Eriugena (9th C).

2. *"God is utterly transcendent, totally ineffable, indescribable and incapable of being conceptualised by the human mind."* Hick on Dionysius

3. *"Perhaps a more balanced approach [than complete reliance on the VN] would be to argue that we need both the via negativa and the via positiva."* Wilkinson and Campbell

4. *"The negative way is the way of darkness, suffering, silence, letting go, and even nothingness."* Sheldrake and Fox

Confusions to avoid

People who take the via negativa approach do think it is possible to talk about God, but God is beyond what we say in human language. To say God is loving does not have any frame of reference, as we only know what loving is in human understanding. God is "beyond assertion." (**DIONYSIUS**) But anything we say about God, even the negative, does not tell us about God, so also "beyond denial", as language is **EQUIVOCAL**. So the experience of God is real, and is what the mystics seek by union with Him, and although the "infinite can penetrate the finite" there can be "no corresponding language statements made" and hence God is ineffable.

THE USE OF ANALOGY

AQUINAS was very familiar with the work of both Dionysius and Maimonides. Aquinas rejected the via negativa because he thought that it was possible to speak positively of God in non-literal and analogical terms. Hence he rejected **EQUIVOCAL LANGUAGE** as it has no link between what we say using our language to describe things available to us (ie something is beautiful or good) and how we use the same language when referring to God.

Does this mean that when we talk about beautiful and good in our language, this means exactly the same when applied to God? This sort of use of language is known as **UNIVOCAL** and Aquinas went on to reject this also, as things do not mean exactly the same when they are used in description of a thing in this world and when used to describe God. "God is strong" and "I am strong" do not mean the same thing.

Aquinas' alternative was to make use of **ANALOGICAL LANGUAGE**, which carries some kind of shared understanding between what it means when describing an object and when that same term is used to describe God. There is some **COMPARISON** that can be made between two different things when using analogy. **WE CAN SAY SOMETHING**. For example, to say a computer is like a brain is to note similarities between those two things, like they both have a kind of electrical circuit, they both receive input and produce output and they both process data, without saying they are the same.

Aquinas goes on to define two types of analogy that can be used. The first is the **ANALOGY OF ATTRIBUTION**. This is when there is a **CAUSAL RELATIONSHIP** that can be described by the terms being used. For example, if someone says that the piece of furniture is good, we can say that the carpenter must be good. Now, we do not mean that the carpenter has a polished finish and finely shaped handles (that would be univocal language); neither do we say that there is no connection between how we are using good to describe the piece of furniture and good to describe the carpenter (that would be equivocal language). We see that there is some causal link between saying that the furniture is good, and that the carpenter is good. **BECAUSE** the carpenter is good, the furniture is good. The example that Aquinas gave is that of a bull's urine. If one sees a sample of the bull's urine and it is healthy (not cloudy etc), then we can **ATTRIBUTE THIS TO THE HEALTH OF THE BULL**. There is a causal link between the two.

Aquinas argued that this meant we can, by the analogy of attribution, begin to **AFFIRM SOME THINGS OF GOD**. As God is the creator of the world, **WE CAN ATTRIBUTE THE GOODNESS OF THE WORLD TO THE GOODNESS OF GOD** in the same way we can say that the good quality of the urine is due to the good quality of the bull.

Aquinas' second use of analogy is the **ANALOGY OF PROPORTION**. This simply means when we use a word like "good", and we say God is good, what we are saying is that **THERE IS A WAY TO BE GOOD THAT BELONGS TO GOD**, just like there is a way for a person to be good that is appropriate for a person. There is an understanding between the use of the words, but there is also a difference, as **EACH IS USED PROPORTIONATELY TO THE SUBJECT**. So, when we say humans are powerful and God is powerful, we are saying that God is powerful in a greater way than humans could ever be.

We are saying that good is what it means for something to act well according to its **NATURE** - for a computer to be good is very different from what it means for an umbrella to be good, but both have their way of being good. This is the way in which Aquinas is using these terms (such as good or powerful), and it has links back to Aristotle's function argument.

So by analogy there are forms of language that can provide some ways of talking about God that carry meaning and understanding.

There is something in common in the terms being used - which is more than there is in equivocal use of language, and affirmative in a way that the via negativa could never be.

RAMSEY also made use of analogy to argue that it is possible to speak meaningfully about God. Ramsey noted that we can use **MODELS** when talking about God. If we say that God is loving, we have a model of loving because we know what loving is in human terms; the example of it we see in human interactions acts as some kind of model and gives us understanding of what loving means.

However, because we are talking about **GOD'S LOVE**, we have to **QUALIFY** our model. The models are useful, but they do not paint the whole picture - they are limited. Whilst humans model love, God is **INFINITELY LOVING**; without this qualification, we are just left with our model of what human love looks like.

This model and qualifier idea can lead to an insight into the quality being spoken about, in this case, the love of God, and Ramsey called such insight a **DISCLOSURE**. At this point, the qualified model has helped take us "beyond" to some disclosure about God. He used this argument to criticise the narrowness of the **VERIFICATION PRINCIPLE**, which, with its focus on empirical facts, did not take account of the empirical meaning found through personal "disclosure experiences".

Strengths

- Analogy avoids **ANTHROPOMORPHISM**, where God is given human qualities, because both Aquinas' analogy of proportion and Ramsey's models and qualifiers avoid saying that "this describes God". They both qualify their use of language when applying things found in human experience to God.

- **POSITIVE** - Analogy enables a person to say something positive of God which might be more appropriate to the experience of most believers than that of the **VN**. At the same time, both Aquinas and Ramsey acknowledge the limited nature of language when used to try to describe God.

- **COMPLEXITY** - By taking human experience as a starting point of reference, Aquinas and Ramsey think that analogy can give insight into complex ideas such as God as all-loving and all-powerful.

Weaknesses

- **ATTRIBUTING EVIL** - Should we not also attribute the evil of the world to God? This would then weaken Aquinas' idea of what type of God he is wishing to put forward by the use of analogy. **HUME** argues that we tend to use whatever analogy supports our existing belief. In looking at the world as it is, what qualities would we attribute to its maker? **DAWKINS** argues that it is the world that would indicate a fight for survival rather than a world which can be attributed to a loving God.

- **ASSUMES SOMETHING** - To use the analogy of attribution assumes that we know something of the nature of God in order for us to say that "a good world" is indicative of "a good God", so this may be confirming what a person already believes. Analogy also "assumes some similarity between the humans and God" (**EYRE**); The opposite conclusion might be equally valid - that God and humans share no similarities.

- **SWINBURNE** has argued that we do not need to use analogy at all, as univocal language is sufficient when talking of God. When we call humans good and God good, we are using the word univocally, which is sufficient, carries meaning and can be understood.

- **BARTH** has criticised analogy because knowledge of God cannot be gained from creation. Knowledge of God by its very nature, argues Barth, is only given by revelation from God.

Key quotes

1. *"It seems that no word can be used literally of God." Aquinas in Summa Theologiae*

2. *"Analogy enables language drawn from the spatio-temporal universe to be applied to a timeless and spaceless God and for this language to be held to be true, but the content of this language is extremely limited." Vardy*

3. *"The most we can say is that: Under the analogy of attribution, God has whatever it takes to create goodness (for instance) in human beings - but we don't know what it is. Under the analogy of proportion, it is true that God is good in whatever way it is appropriate for God to be good. We do not, however, know in what way it is appropriate for God to be good." Vardy*

4. *"Religious language consists of 'disclosure models' that are made up of both analogy and existential depth." Jackson on Ramsey*

Confusions to avoid

Both Aquinas and Ramsey are very clear that the use of analogy is still limited by human language. It would be wrong to say that they think they have found a way in which God can be adequately described. If you said that the way Usain Bolt runs is similar to the way in which an arrow leaves the bow and reaches its target, you are not saying that Bolt is a thin aluminium alloy shaft attached to an arrowhead fired from a 60 pound bow. What you are saying is that the speed with which he is released from the blocks has similarities to the way in which the arrow is fired from the bow, as is the way in which he runs straight and true, and with speed, towards a final target. The archery analogy "points towards"; it helps provide a comparison which highlights similar features between one thing and another.

THE USE OF MYTH

A **MYTH** is a story which conveys a religious belief or truth, or which points to a deeper reality, but is not factually true. A myth can include the use of symbols or metaphors or other literary devices, which are used to convey important truth(s) or unfold a worldview. Myths often deal with issues of ultimate significance such as the creation of the world, human identity, suffering, evil, morality and purpose.

Many Christians think that the **CREATION STORIES** are not meant to be read in a factual manner, but as myth, and are attempts by the writer or writers to point the reader towards things like structure within the universe, rhythm and order within creation, a creator who desires a relationship with humanity and the idea of work being part of the purpose of mankind. To ask whether a myth is "true" in a historical or scientific sense is the wrong question, just as one would not ask if poetry is "true".

As creation stories convey "truths" about the worldview of that community, it could be argued that there is **COGNITIVE MEANING** contained within them and this will be important when we come to study the **VERIFICATION PRINCIPLE** and how that principle seeks to measure how meaning is carried in language.

In the 20th C **BULTMANN** argued that the New Testament must be **DEMYTHOLOGISED** if truth is to be discovered in it. Scientific understanding will not allow us to read scripture, and accounts such as a literal virgin birth, as previous generations did, which was in a very simplistic, "supernatural" and non-scientific way. The writers of the Gospels who weave their stories around the life of Jesus did so because they wanted to portray Jesus as having miraculous powers and draw the reader towards that conclusion, which would then require a response to

Jesus. They would also attach details to the stories about Jesus to emphasise the message they were trying to convey, such as when they describe Jesus as conversing with a prostitute, or when they place Pharisees (religious rulers of the day) together with "sinners", both of which would never have occurred. Bultmann argues that these little stories, created for emphasis of the message of Christ, are not essential for the message; there is a need for these accounts to be demythologised in order to return to the message of Christ.

WILKINSON and **CAMPBELL** note that "perhaps Bultmann's approach is mistaken. Rather than stripping out the myths from Scripture, perhaps the task of the believer might not be to deny that the myths are myth, but rather to accept that they are myths and to try to discern what truths they might contain".

Strengths

- **TRUE MEANING** - The use of myth utilises story and a more flowing, lively and memorable narrative when trying to convey truths that might not fit other mediums. This might broaden our understanding of truths which could not be outlined in a factual manner but which nonetheless carry meaning.

- **STORY -** There is a recent move to retell history such as the events of the Tudor Court, as story, and, in these stories, factual truth is used where it suits the story, but the fabrication of other details adds to the overall message the historian is trying to get across. However, it could be argued that the use of the word myth is inappropriate here, as there is still enough factual history in the retelling of the Tudor period for example, unlike the creation myths, which for many readers contain very little, or even no, factual truth at all.

- **MORAL IMPETUS** - Religious language, **Braithwaite** argues, is meant to assert moral claims which express the desire to act in a certain way. In this way, they carry meaning in a wider way than can be measured by the **VERIFICATION OR FALSIFICATION THEORIES**. Braithwaite claims that the stories in which the truth is outlined give **MORAL IMPETUS** for how people should live towards one another, and do not need to be true for the "religious person to … resolve to live a certain way of life" (**JORDAN** et al) after listening to the truths contained within them.

Weaknesses

- **CHALLENGE OF SCIENCE** - The stories may have fitted a world in which the beginning of the universe was a mystery, but now we have the theory of the Big Bang, it is questionable whether the use of myth is still needed to convey truths or, in the words of **WILKINSON** and **CAMPBELL**, "fill gaps" which now no longer need filling.

- **CULTURALLY DETERMINED** - "Mythological imagery has a tendency to be culturally determined." (**AHLUWALIA**) Many religious believers want to say that there are central truths, or even a central Truth, that their sacred text is conveying, and these core elements might get missed or misinterpreted if myth is the medium in which those truths are told. "If a myth is just a made-up story like a fable, then it does not communicate any truths about God." (**TAYLOR**)

- **COMPETING MYTHS** - "There is no agreed criteria for judging which myth communicates truth." (**TAYLOR**)

Napoleon once noted that history is the lies of the winner; how do we know that the myths that have survived are not those from the dominant worldview? Do such stories still contain truths or are they more like propaganda? Myths may change over time to respond to current concerns so that it is difficult to assess whether or not they contain eternal truths. Taylor notes that an example of this is how in recent years Christians have interpreted the "dominion over nature" idea portrayed in the creation myth as containing the instruction to "steward" (caretake) creation, which has a very different connotation from that of dominion.

- **FLEW** might argue that it is convenient how stories in the Bible that were once held to be factually true, such as the creation story or that of Noah's ark, are now viewed as mythological, and carrying "deeper-than-literal" truth. If this is the case, have Christians who take this line shifted the goalposts as it were, and maintained the truth of holy scripture but by a disingenuous re-reading of text? Is this "death by a thousand qualifications"? Christians might reply that this is now a significantly better way of reading the text, which is more true to the writer's intentions. But in doing so, have they reduced sacred text to a series of nice pieces of advice, rather than the giving of Truth (with a capital, realist T)? Yet many Christians do not read the creation story or that of Noah and other stories, as myth, but as literally true.

Key quotes

1. *"The more real things get, the more like myths they become."* Fassbinder

2. *"The miracle stories added later should be regarded as statements of faith, stories told in the early Church. This is not a problem for Bultmann as the literal truth of these accounts is unimportant to the teaching (or kerygma) of Jesus."* Eyre et al

3. *"Myths are stories that express meaning, morality or motivation. Whether they are true or not is irrelevant."* Shermer

4. *"Through myth, believers are able to communicate something positive about God, without having to resort to the via negativa."* Ahluwalia

5. *"Because philosophy arises from awe, a philosopher is bound in his way to be a lover of myths and poetic fables. Poets and philosophers are alike in being big with wonder."* Aquinas

6. *"Myths and creeds are heroic struggles to comprehend the truth in the world."* Adams

7. *"It is a sure sign that a culture has reached a dead end when it is no longer intrigued by its myths."* Marcus

8. *"Old myths, old gods, old heroes have never died. They are only sleeping at the bottom of our mind, waiting for our call. We have need for them. They represent the wisdom of our race."* Kunitz

Confusions to avoid

A clear definition of myth needs to be used when writing about this use of religious language. Myth as "old wives' tales" is not the way in which the term is understood in theology and by religious believers.

There is a need for understanding of how different parts of sacred text are interpreted in different ways, so that when a believer says that the creation story is myth, this does not mean that a) it is less important than other parts of scripture or that b) the rest of the text is myth. Many Christians argue that there are different genres in scripture, such as myth, history, poetry, prophecy etc, and the reading of each in a particular way is respectful of literary interpretation.

THE USE OF SYMBOL

20th C philosopher **PAUL TILLICH** wrote extensively about the use of **SYMBOL** in religious language, and how such could carry meaning.

Tillich argued that God is the **GROUND OF ALL BEING**, or **BEING ITSELF**. A crude illustration might help explain what Tillich meant by this: If you imagine a number of things on a shopping list, such as carrots, milk and tea bags, God is not one more thing on the list like any other object, which could or could not exist (many theologians have criticised **DAWKINS** for his description of God as one more thing on the list of contingent things). God is the list itself - God is the ground of all other things, being itself. For Tillich, God is the **ULTIMATE CONCERN**. If this is so, how is it possible to speak of, or journey towards, such Being (not "a being")?

For Tillich, **SYMBOLS** help us in this journey as they point "**BEYOND THEMSELVES**" and "open up new levels of reality". Just as a flag of a country can no longer be viewed by the winning athlete who sees it raised at the Olympics as a piece of coloured cloth but as something that seems to take them on a journey of pride in themselves, their country and all that the flag means and represents, so a symbol such as bread and wine takes a person beyond the elements of bread and wine to ultimate reality, to being itself.

An example of a symbol is water, which is used in many religions. When water is used in a religious ritual, it is a symbol that enables those who are immersed in it to have the experience of purity or spiritual cleansing, perhaps even a sense of a fresh beginning. Now the water does not and cannot actually provide those things, but rather symbolises or points towards Being itself, which can be accessed through this participatory symbol. The way in which religious language is understood, and being used here, is both **EVOCATIVE** and **POETIC**, but Tillich is clearly claiming that it also carries some **COGNITIVE, IF NOT LITERAL, MEANING**.

Tillich used examples such as music and painting to help us understand how symbols move us towards a deeper reality, releasing in the observer something which only that symbol could do. However, to really understand Tillich it is necessary to realise that **STATEMENTS** about God, such as "God is love", are symbolic too; it is not just physical objects that act as symbols but language has to be symbolic when talking of God as he is Being Itself (not just another being).

EYRE et al explain this idea when they write that whilst "we are familiar with religious symbols such as the cross or the bread and wine ... what Tillich is suggesting is that even statements such as 'God is good' are symbolic rather than literal ... Tillich refers to God as 'the ground of being', and suggests that this is the only non-symbolic statement that can be made about God". Here Tillich is meaning that statements about God are symbolic and participate in the reality of God, without meaning that language has ever captured what God is in a literal way. (Incidentally, this is indication of the difference between a symbol and a sign, the latter only imparting one message to the reader, such as "no entry", or a 60mph speed limit, and not pointing towards, or participating in, anything beyond itself).

To summarise Tillich and religious language - a symbol:

1. elicits a response

2. evokes participation in the intended meaning (be careful here - look at the third quotation below)

3. points to something beyond itself

4. may be understood on a number of levels.

Strengths

- **UNIVERSAL** - We widely use symbols in art, poetry or music to point us to something which is difficult to express, and this "beyond" to which it points does carry meaning for us.

- **AVOIDS ANTHROPOMORPHISM** - The symbols of God's power and other attributes are not interpreted in ways which "describe" God or bring Him down to a human level; the opposite happens as symbols point towards Being itself rather than a being who is like a person.

- **METAPHORIC** - It could be argued that we do use language in a symbolic or metaphoric way all the time. When we say that we could murder a cup of tea, we are not meaning that literally, but symbolically pointing towards the fact of our thirst. **AHLUWALIA** points out that when we say God hears our prayers, we do not mean that he literally does, as he has no ears, but the statement symbolises a characteristic of God (concern).

Weaknesses

- **NON-COGNITIVE** - Symbols enable us to delve deeper into human experience rather than act as something that point us to any ultimate reality in which they participate. **EYRE** et al note that this is how **RANDALL** interprets symbol. The symbol does not carry any cognitive meaning, but is entirely non-cognitive. A flag might not actually represent anything other than citizens' ideas about the country, rather than anything "in reality". Postmodernists might argue that any reality is carried in the words themselves and not anything that lies behind them.

- **AMBIGUOUS** - Hick has questioned what Tillich means when he argues that a symbol "participates" in the thing towards which it points. When Tillich talks about participation, he means that the symbol "somehow represents the event and gives access to a deeper level of understanding of the event", **(TAYLOR)** citing Tillich's example of music that takes us to reality beyond the actual notes to communicate feelings and emotions and even evoke beliefs. How does the physical symbol participate in the metaphysical reality towards which Tillich argues it points?

- **MEANINGLESS** - What meaning does religious language have if it is symbolic and not literal? Is it actually saying anything of meaning? And even if such might carry meaning, who is to know if that meaning is correct, as what the symbol points towards is not available to us through experience?

Issues arising

- How successfully has religion responded to the verification and falsification theory?

- Is it possible to talk meaningfully about God?

- How successful are the various explanations of the nature of religious language?

Key quotes

1. *"Symbolic language alone is able to express the ultimate because it transcends the capacity of any finite reality to express it directly." Tillich*

2. *"When the Bible speaks of the kingdom of God, the symbol of a kingdom is concerned with the ultimate reality of God's power and rule." Jordan et al.*

3. *"Symbols are meaningful on account of their relationship to the ultimate. There is an idolatrous tendency to confuse the symbol (eg a holy person, book, doctrine, or ritual) with the ultimate." Tillich*

4.   *"Religion is the state of being grasped by an ultimate concern, a concern which qualifies all other concerns as preliminary and which itself contains the answer to the question of the meaning of our life." Tillich*

Confusions to avoid

Signs do not participate in the reality of that to which they point, and can be replaced "for reasons of convention or expediency". Symbols do participate and also "cannot be replaced except after an historic catastrophe that changes the reality of the nation which it symbolises". (Tillich)

THE VERIFICATION PRINCIPLE (VP)

Having studied ways in which it is proposed that religious language carries meaning, the **VP** puts forward a test to see if in fact that is the case.

From 1907 onwards a group of philosophers who had a scientific background attempted to define how meaning is carried in language and, according to **PHELAN**, "to eliminate metaphysics from philosophy". This group, known as the **VIENNA CIRCLE**, was influenced by **WITTGENSTEIN'S** proposal that the meaning of a proposition being put forward lay in knowing what is pictured by those words. The circle also built on the work of **HUME**, who had argued that statements only contain meaning if they are **ANALYTIC, A PRIORI AND NECESSARY** or **SYNTHETIC, A POSTERIORI AND CONTINGENT**. This distinction became known as **HUME'S FORK**. The Vienna Circle saw themselves as guardians of language in judging what statements carried meaning; the metaphysical did not, as it did not meet the criteria outlined by either Wittgenstein or Hume.

AJ AYER, who must have impressed his first wife by visiting the Vienna Circle whilst on honeymoon in 1932, approved of the rigorous test that the VP put towards language, and he felt that it helped philosophy to have clear guidelines concerning what language carries meaning and what doesn't. Building on the work of the Vienna Circle, Ayer published Language, Logic and Truth at the age of 25, and this became enormously popular as a classical definition of the Circle's **LOGICAL POSITIVISM**, whereby meaning is established in language.

Within this work, Ayer stated that a statement only carried meaning if it was: a **TAUTOLOGY** - true by definition (bachelors are unmarried men, which is an a priori statement), or **VERIFIABLE IN PRINCIPLE** by evidence (there is life on at least one other planet - there might not be, but, in principle with the development of technology, we could one day find out, ie verify it using our senses; this is an a posteriori statement).

Ayer's addition of the words **IN PRINCIPLE** to the verification criteria is often seen as progression from the very strict definition of meaning that was arrived at by the VP. The verification demanded by the Vienna Circle required direct observation of an event for it to have any meaning, which automatically ruled out any historical events. Ayer's **VERIFICATION IN PRINCIPLE** meant that historical and future events could in principle be verified. Ayer used an illustration from **SCHLICK**, a member of the Vienna Circle, to make this point when he suggested that one day we may be able to verify if "there are mountains on the far side of the moon". As such a statement was verifiable in principle it carried meaning.

In his first edition of Language, Logic and Truth, Ayer also wrote of a type of verification called **WEAK VERIFICATION**, in which he argued that there are general laws which cover many individual cases. To check that "a body tends to expand when heated" is impossible on a case by case basis, ie, impossible to verify; however, this is most probably the case, and the principle of weak verification accepts that there is meaning in such statements. This was different to **STRONG VERIFICATION**, which was when a statement was conclusively verified by sense-experience and observation.

Later, following much criticism of these criteria, Ayer would reject the strong and weak verification distinction, suggesting that the latter allowed for too many statements to carry meaning, whilst strong verification was too difficult a demand for most statements. He went on to develop a different distinction by arguing for **DIRECTLY AND INDIRECTLY VERIFIABLE OBSERVATION STATEMENTS**. Direct verification was possible where a person could check that, for example, "the tide is out at Weston-super-Mare", or that "exit signs are green" - these are verifiable by observation. Indirect observations are statements about things which cannot be directly observed. **TAYLOR**, in interpreting Ayer's criteria, describes these statements as those that "could be verified if other directly verifiable evidence could support it". This would be the case, for example, with the observation of quarks, where all the evidence of other observable things points to their existence, even though quarks themselves are not directly observable.

Ayer makes clear that any religious or metaphysical statements fail the test as they a) are not tautological in nature or b) ever verifiable, observable, or supported by other direct observation statements. Thus, for Ayer, **METAPHYSICAL** language is **MEANINGLESS**. While disciplines such as history and science put forward either tautologies or propositions that are verifiable, metaphysical language (which includes religious language claims for God) does not meet such a standard. They are "factual non-sense", as there is actually no way of verifying such claims.

Ayer is not saying that religious language is false - it is neither true nor false, as for something to be verified as true or false it has to have meaning, and such meaning comes through empirical verification of some sort. The statement "all giraffes have six legs" is false, but it is meaningful as it can be verified as true or false by observation. God exists (or God does not exist) is never verifiable; there are no means by which we can verify statements about God as true or false and hence they carry no factual meaning or significance.

Strengths

- **RIGOROUS** - The attempt to define what is meaningful and meaningless could be seen as useful in helping to filter out statements that seem to be philosophically valid but in fact do not actually say anything. As **COLE** notes, Ayer felt that "through the misuse of language people assumed that because a word existed there must be some corresponding reality". Ayer has provided a useful check to counter absurd claims.

- **REVISED** - Ayer's revision of the verification principle so that a statement can carry meaning if its claim can be verified in principle can be seen as both a strength and a weakness. It shows a philosopher who is willing to revise his theory, but this change might critically weaken what the verification principle is trying to achieve.

Weaknesses

- **FAILS ITS OWN TEST** - The Verification Principle does not carry any meaning according to its own criteria. The VP itself is not analytical, and nor could any empirical evidence be provided to verify it. By its own standards therefore, the VP is itself meaningless. So how can its own claims can be true?

- **VERIFICATION IS POSSIBLE** - The VP's rejection of any meaning in religious and metaphysical language is countered by **HICK** who suggests it might be possible to verify the claims of religion at the end of our lives. He uses the parable in which two people journey along a road, one believing that it leads to a celestial city and the other that it is leading nowhere. One of these two will be correct, but the verification of which view is correct is not possible until after death. This is known as **ESCHATALOGICAL VERIFICATION** and meets the "verifiable in principle" condition.

- **EVIDENCE** - It is difficult to know what sort of evidence counts when trying to meet the weak verification principle. What evidence is admissible? What if many people claim to have had a religious experience - does this provide empirical evidence? Can God be ruled out as the cause? With regard to the clause "verifiable in principle" **WARD** has noted that the existence of God is verifiable in principle by God himself.

- **ASSUMES** that the scientific method is the only way of assessing meaning in language. This is not argued for, and thus is an assertion which there is no obligation to accept.

Key quotes

1. *"No statement which refers to a 'reality' transcending the limits of all possible sense-experience can possibly have any literal significance." Ayer*

2. *"A sentence is factually significant ... if, and only if [a person] knows ... what observations would lead him, under certain conditions, to accept the proposition as being true, or reject it as being false." Ayer*

3. *"A proposition is ... verifiable in the strong sense of the term if, and only if, its truth could be conclusively established ... But it is verifiable in the weak sense if it is possible for experience to render it probable."* Ayer

4. *"We ... define a metaphysical sentence as a sentence which purports to express a genuine proposition, but does, in fact, express neither a tautology nor an empirical hypothesis. And as tautologies and empirical hypotheses form the entire class of significant propositions, we are justified in concluding that all metaphysical assertions are nonsensical."* Ayer

5. *"If we take in our hand any volume; of divinity or school metaphysics, for instance, let us ask, Does it contain any abstract reasoning containing quantity or number? No. Does it contain any experimental reasoning, concerning matter of fact or existence? No. Commit it to the flames: for it can contain nothing but sophistry and illusion."* Hume

6. *"The Verification Principle eventually died the death of a thousand cuts."* Phelan

Confusions to avoid

Ayer is not saying that the statement "God exists" is false. He is saying that any statements about God are statements that cannot be **VERIFIED** (even the agnostic who says "I don't know if God exists" is putting forward his lack of knowledge about God as a meaningful proposition, when such a question could never be meaningful for Ayer). The purpose of the Logical Positivists is to create a method of verification which decides if a statement carries meaning, not if that statement is true or false - that requires secondary research to go and see if the statement is true (eg giraffes have six legs). To make this assessment Ayer argues that the VP is the necessary tool. Statements about God "fail" the test proposed by the VP.

THE FALSIFICATION PRINCIPLE

POPPER rejected the findings of the Logical Positivists and argued that the VP was bad science. He proposed that science should not be looking for continual verifications of its propositions, but rather **FALSIFICATIONS**. He used the example of Freudian psychology to explain this; when Freud argues that difficulties in adult life stem from our traumatic experiences in childhood, this is easy to verify as it is so wide a proposition, and Freud does exactly this when he suggests that every person requires psychiatric counselling. However, what marks real science out from what Popper calls pseudo-science is that a proposition should be able to be falsified. The VP might suggest "there will be sunshine somewhere tomorrow" whereas the FP will suggest "there will be thunder over Birmingham at 2pm tomorrow" - the latter is better because it puts forward something specific that can be falsified; the former can hardly fail and is irrefutable, but this is bad science, not good.

FLEW built on the FP to criticise religious language as non-falsifiable, and because it is, statements such as "God exists" carry no meaning. Flew uses the parable provided by **WISDOM**, in which he describes two people who come across a clearing in the jungle, where there are both flowers and weeds. One person argues that it is tended by a gardener while the other argues that there is no such gardener. The latter suggests that they watch for the gardener's appearance and even sets up elaborate traps and bloodhounds who would smell the gardener if he came in the night. No gardener appears, but the person who believes a gardener comes is not convinced that this has shown there is not a gardener. He suggests that the gardener is invisible, intangible, soundless and even scentless. The unbelieving explorer asks his friend who believes in such a gardener how his gardener differs from there being no gardener at all.

If a believer claims that God is love and someone responds by saying that a loving God would not allow children to die of cancer, the believer might reply that this is because of "God's bigger plan for us". Flew argues therefore that there is little difference between their belief in God and the belief the traveller had about the invisible gardener, and thus no difference between what they are claiming about God and there being no God at all. Belief must **ASSERT** something, and if it asserts something it must **DENY** or **RULE OUT** something too. If it does not, and keeps making exceptions, then it "dies the death of a thousand qualifications". (**FLEW**) As **PHELAN** writes, Flew is asking for, "details of a situation in which belief in God would be untenable; the situation need not be real but simply hypothetical". Without providing such, religious language is **UNFALSIFIABLE** and thus is not putting forward a genuine assertion which is of any significant factual importance.

HARE devised the parable about a man who is convinced that his university teachers are out to kill him, despite evidence against this, such as his teachers' kindness. His entire life, behaviour and reading of events around him are shaped by this conviction, which Hare calls a "**BLIK**". Hare argues that bliks carry deep meaning and they are widespread in the human community, like some kind of psychological conditioning. No one is without some kind of unfalsifiable blik which makes deep sense to us and through which we interpret the world. Hare argues that religious language does not make factual claims but imparts knowledge nonetheless, through the way it influences people's view of the world.

Flew responded to Hare by saying that religious believers are claiming more than he thinks, and are not just saying that their blik is one of many. What believers are claiming is something about the cosmos, in a **REALIST** sense; they claim to be making assertions, which is what Hare fails to realise. If they are making assertions, Flew argues that these must be open to falsification (which they aren't).

A further response to Hare was provided by both **EVANS** and **HICK**, who argued that Hare makes a mistake in writing about bliks being right or wrong or sane or insane; if there is no way of falsifying them, then there is no way of judging what is a right or wrong, sane or insane blik.

A further parable in response to Flew was provided by **MITCHELL**. A French resistance fighter in **WWII** meets a Stranger who says that he is on the side of the resistance, and who convinces the resistance fighter so much that he trusts him. However, the Stranger tells the resistance fighter that at times his behaviour will look at though he is on the side of the German Gestapo. Despite some evidence that would shake his trust, the fighter, who represents the religious believer, maintains his faith in the Stranger, who represents God. He was so impressed by his initial meeting with him that there is enough to maintain his belief, even when the evidence against such belief seems quite powerful.

Mitchell maintains that the person's belief in the personal character of the Stranger is sufficient to enable the believer to sustain faith; religious belief has a quality, depth and reason to it that a believer will not simply abandon when difficult times come, and he argues that Flew has not correctly understood how religious belief operates.

In summary:

- **FLEW** argues that statements about God are not genuine scientific assertions as they cannot be falsified.

- **HARE** argues that religious beliefs, like bliks, are unfalsifiable but carry meaning.

- **MITCHELL** argues that the believer is aware of problems that would count against his belief, but these do not provide sufficient reasons to discard faith.

Strengths

- **TRUE TO SCIENCE** - Many have argued that **POPPER's** criteria for marking science from pseudo-science was a much more useful and valid move than looking for continual verification of a proposition, which actually does not move scientific understanding on.

- **EVALUATIVE** - Flew challenges the believer to evaluate what is being claimed in such statements such as "God is love" or "God has a plan"; are such factual claims?

Weaknesses

- **AHLUWALIA** - Suggests that Flew's "confidence in empirical evidence as the final test of meaning is, in itself, unfalsifiable".

- **PHELAN** writes that the evidence required by Flew's falsifying test would have to be a) unambiguous, b) identifiable by everyone and c) non-jargonistic, and it is not clear if religious language works like that, or whether such is possible. He notes that it would be possible to falsify the belief that there is a loving God if it could be proved that the world works ultimately against our welfare, but that is a difficult challenge.

Key quotes

1. *"Hare is echoing Wittgenstein's point that religious beliefs are used to evaluate reality, rather than something that one checks against reality."* Phelan

2. *"Metaphysical claims about the existence and nature of God are obviously not open to empirical verification or falsification since God is not an empirically observable object."* Brummer

3. *"To say that religious sentences are not reducible to scientific assertions is a wholly separate question from whether they are true or false."* Wilkinson and Campbell

4. *"By saying that God is invisible, soundless, incorporeal and so on, there is very little difference between our definition of God and our definition of nothingness; we argue God out of existence by 'a thousand qualifications'."* Ahluwalia

Confusions to avoid

- Do not just list the many scholars who have contributed to the debate concerning the VP and the FP. The parables given by the different philosophers were illustrative of major criticisms and you must use them in this way; if you do not draw out the meaning and expand this, then retelling the parable itself will not gain you marks.

- Flew is not talking about the meaningfulness of religious language; he is arguing that the FP is a test of whether something is making a scientific assertion or not. Religious language does not make a scientific assertion because it cannot be falsified, which genuine assertions can be. Religious language may have meaning in other ways.

- Note that Hick's eschatological verification might meet the qualification of the weak verification principle, in that it is possible to suggest that the existence of God is verifiable in principle, post death. However it is impossible to falsify such a claim. Hick was actually pointing out the limitations of the falsification theory, that whilst some things can be verified, such as the eschatological celestial city, they cannot necessarily be falsified.

WITTGENSTEIN'S LANGUAGE GAMES

WITTGENSTEIN did not so much look at meaning of language but how language is used. Words, when used within their "game", do not simply describe an object, but have a **FUNCTION** or **USE**, like **TOOLS**, which is how Wittgenstein described and viewed words. There are many "language games", such as rugby or music, and Wittgenstein's own example is that of chess, where language such as "move pawn to E4" makes sense, carries meaning and performs a function within the rules of the chess language game. Within that language game, if someone gave an instruction to move the pawn three spaces to the left, then that would be "nonsense", literally of no sense, as the instruction does not follow the rules of that particular language game. Similarly, if someone said, pick up the ball and run ten metres, that language is not appropriate or used in the chess game.

If you are reading this in class, there will be many language games going on in the school, such as in the Physics classroom, or in PE. Even individual words such as "mass" will have different understandings within the different games in which they are used - if mass is being taught in Physics it will have a very different meaning than when taught in an RE lesson about Roman Catholic practice. To understand the meaning of the language, you must look at the activity that it refers to within its game.

These language games are part of life; when we joke or give thanks, we participate in a game that has particular rules. Language games are the way in which we enter into understanding of the world. Wittgenstein developed this idea further when outlining how speaking is a "**FORM OF LIFE**" shared with others; **BURNS** and **LAW** describe a form of life as "the activity with which a language game is associated" so that "talk of the love of God must be understood not only in the context of other things that are said about God, but also by looking at what it means in practice".

Because these games are forms of life, language is never private as it takes place and has meaning and function within its game, and develops within that setting. Wittgenstein would therefore reject any ideas that we can use language in a private capacity, such as carried out by Descartes and his claim: "I think therefore I am." It would appear that Descartes thinks such a claim is formed by the private use of language whereas language is always a public discourse for Wittgenstein, and it is from such use in its form of life that it gains its meaning.

In outlining this philosophy, Wittgenstein deliberately moved away from his earlier support of the Logical Positivist's definition of meaning in language. Later Wittgensteinian philosophy allows for religious language to have meaning within its game, although it is followers of Wittgenstein, such as **PHILLIPS**, rather than Wittgenstein himself, who have developed his theory with reference to religious language. The statement "God is love" is very meaningful within the group or game in which that sort of language is used, whilst not understood by those outside that particular game. Therefore, it is not possible to offer simple verification or falsification tests to religious language, or indeed, any other language; these sorts of tests may be more relevant to the physical world, as **TAYLOR** notes, but cannot assess meaning in language. Language carries significance and meaning within the game through its use.

Wittgenstein argued that philosophical problems arise when "language goes on holiday". For example, if we take the word "soul" and think that we are talking about some physical object, then we are applying the wrong rules to it, and the "physical" game rules do not apply in this instance.

Strengths

- **TRUE TO LANGUAGE** - The VP and The FP have limited use in explaining how the metaphysical is deeply meaningful, which is what religious language purports to be.

- **TRUE TO RELIGIOUS LIFE** - As **TAYLOR** notes, "for many religious believers, religion is not a philosophical enquiry into the nature of belief, but a shared community life, culture, identity and practices".

Weaknesses

- **ANTI-REALISM** - Wittgenstein has removed any **REALIST** claims that religious believers would want to make, such as "Jesus died for the sins of everyone". Christians would want to assert this as **TRUE**, as such statements **CORRESPOND** to an actual truth; they are not just assertions that make sense within the community of believers in a way which **COHERES** with other language that is used within the game.

- **DIALOGUE IMPOSSIBLE** between people on two sides of an argument: the believer and the atheist. Language does not make sense just within its own game, but has universal meaning.

- **CIRCULAR** - Wittgenstein's proposal is circular. Words take their meaning from the language game which they are in, and the game gets its meaning from the words from which it is constructed.

Key quotes

1. *"The limits of my language mean the limits of my world."*
   Wittgenstein

2. *"Don't ask for the meaning, ask for the use." Wittgenstein*

3. *"We cannot get 'outside' the games to ask the 'real' meaning of words. We can only play another game." Wilkinson and Campbell*

4. *"The philosopher's task is to describe the way we use language, not to ask questions about whether or not things exist." Burns and Law*

Confusions to avoid

- The meaning of language is found through its use in its form of life rather than its description of any reality. The issue here is if this anti-realist understanding is an accurate representation of what believers are saying when they make such statements as "God is love".

- Do not say that Wittgenstein thinks each language game describes reality, even a reality that makes sense within that game; instead, each language game is using words in a particular and internally coherent way. No language is either "true" or "false" for Wittgenstein.

GET MORE HELP

Get more help with religious language by using the links below:

http://i-pu.sh/B4M01N23

Body, Soul & Personal Identity

Key terms

- **DUALISM** - The belief that the mind/soul and the body are separate entities.

- **HADITH** - The traditions and reported sayings of the Prophet Muhammad. Second to the Qur'an, it provides authority of action for Muslims.

- **IMMORTALITY** - The ability to live forever.

- **MATERIALISM** - The belief that the mind/soul and the body are not separate entities. Sometimes called **MONISM**.

- **RESURRECTION** - The act of rising from the dead or returning to life. This can be where the whole body returns to life or a spiritual resurrection of the soul.

Please support our learning community by not photocopying without a licence

THE RELATIONSHIP BETWEEN THE BODY AND SOUL

For millennia people have questioned whether there is anything that survives after death. For some psychologists and anthropologists the desire for an afterlife is caused by fear of death - in order to cope with the inevitability of life (death) humanity has created a safety net. For the major world faiths this is not the case. Judaism, Christianity and Islam argue for the existence of an afterlife that is a reward for positive actions on Earth, whilst Hinduism and Buddhism state that life after death will continue until we are released from suffering. Philosophers and theologians differ on an understanding of what it is that continues, and this topic explores the relationship between the body, soul and personal identity.

BELIEFS ABOUT THE NATURE OF THE SOUL

Beliefs about the soul can be divided into two categories - **MATERIALISM** and **DUALISM**. Dualists argue that the body is **SEPARATE** from the soul and that the soul has unique features which mean that it can survive the death of the body. Materialists believe that the body and the soul exist as one and that there can be no survival after death.

DUALISM

Most **DUALISTS** believe that the soul is what individuates each human. It contains their thoughts and beliefs. The "I" and your **PERSONAL IDENTITY** are distinct from the body.

PLATO was a dualist. He believed in two realities: the "world of objects" and the "world of the forms". The physical realm that we live in is the "world of objects". All things in this world are **REFLECTIONS** of the true and immortal reality; the "world of the forms". The human mind or soul, because it contains abstract ideas and beliefs, is unlike the rest of the physical world and belongs to the world of the **FORMS**. All things in this world "participate" in their equivalent Form. Beautiful things "participate" in the Form of Beauty, whilst things that are good "participate" in the Form of the Good. The soul "participates" in the Form of Life and as such, it is immortal and becomes separated from the body when the body dies. While the body is alive the soul "remembers" its existence in the world of the forms. This is how a person gains knowledge, and throughout life the soul strives to return to the immortal realm. Through philosophy a person can free themselves from ignorance and understand their true reality. "Ordinary people seem not to realise that those who really apply themselves in the proper way to philosophy are directly and of their own accord preparing themselves for death and dying." (**PLATO**)

For Plato, the rational part of a human's mind is what continues. This "thinking essence" is a person's **PERSONAL IDENTITY**. The "I" continues after death.

Plato used **THE ALLEGORY OF THE CAVE** to highlight the relationship between the soul and the "world of the forms". In this allegory a prisoner escapes from his imprisonment in a cave where he has been his entire life. As he struggles to the surface, a metaphor for the souls desire to rejoin the Forms, he learns that his previous existence has been a **SHADOW** of the real world. Finally, he reaches the surface and sees the sun (the Form of the Good) and he is enlightened to true knowledge. This is a metaphor for the relationship of the Forms to the soul. Through philosophy we can overcome ignorance and gain clarity. This enables the soul to better remember the eternal truths that it had access to and become more fulfilled.

ARISTOTLE had a different view to **PLATO**. He believed all living things have a **SOUL** which turns the body of the creature into a "living" organism. He writes: "Suppose that the eye were an animal - sight would have been its soul, for sight is the substance or essence of the eye which corresponds to the formula, the eye being merely the matter of seeing; when seeing is removed the eye is no longer an eye, except in name." (**ARISTOTLE**)

Human's souls are **INTELLECTUAL** or **THINKING** souls, as opposed to the **SENSORY** soul of animals. This "thinking" soul enables humans to grasp knowledge and eternal truths. Importantly the soul, although distinct from the body, is not separate - it gives the body its form.

Despite this **DUALISM**, **ARISTOTLE** did not believe that the **SOUL** could exist separate from the body. He writes: "The soul does not exist without a body and yet is not itself a kind of body. For it is not a body, but something which belongs to a body, and for this reason exists in a body, and in a body of such-and-such a kind." Because they are not separate the soul cannot be **IMMORTAL** and life after death is not possible.

AQUINAS, following **ARISTOTLE**, claimed that the soul gives the body life. He called it **ANIMA** because it animates the body. Only things which are divisible can decay and change. The soul is **INDIVISIBLE** and does not change. Thus it can survive death. The soul individuates the body. As the body dies the soul continues as the **PERSONAL IDENTITY** of the body.

RENÉ DESCARTES believed that humans are defined by their ability to think. He famously said "I think, therefore I am". Self-consciousness makes humans unique from animals. The body is a physical substance whilst the mind is non-physical, "whose whole essence is to think". Our thoughts and beliefs are what define our identity; they are the "I", and because the mind/soul is a non-physical substance it can survive death.

DESCARTES used the term **MIND** and **SOUL** interchangeably. Physical rules do not apply to the mind. It does not age or change, and does not die. These are features of the body. This mind/body dualism means that when the body dies the two can separate and the soul can continue to live with God after death. This is an **INTERACTIONIST** view of mind and body. The mind interacts with and controls the body. Descartes believed this happened through the **PINEAL GLAND** in the brain.

The **JUDAEO-CHRISTIAN** (and particularly the **CHRISTIAN**) belief argues for a dualism of mind and body. The Bible teaches that humans have a soul that was created by God and is distinct from the body. "The Lord God formed the man of dust from the ground and breathed into his nostrils the breath of life, and the man became a living creature." (Genesis 2:7) The breath of life is added after the physical body and animates the body.

Within this tradition, whether a soul survives death is dependent on God's **JUDGEMENT**. The concept of personal identity is also important, as an individual is judged solely on their own actions and not on the actions of another. "The son shall not suffer for the iniquity of the father, nor the father suffer for the iniquity of the son." (Ezekiel 18:20)

Christianity based on the teaching of Jesus takes this further. "In my Father's house are many rooms. If it were not so, would I have told you that I go to prepare a place for you?" (John 14:2) Jesus taught that the afterlife exists and the individual personal soul will continue after death.

In the **PARABLE OF THE SHEEP AND THE GOATS** he states that positive judgement is reliant on individuals acting with love. "When the

Son of Man comes in his glory, and all the angels with him, then he will sit on his glorious throne. Before him will be gathered all the nations, and he will separate people one from another as a shepherd separates the sheep from the goats. (Matthew 25:31-33)

PAUL claims that evidence for the afterlife rests with the fact of Jesus' resurrection. If Jesus were not resurrected then humans would not be resurrected. "For if the dead are not raised, not even Christ has been raised. And if Christ has not been raised, your faith is futile and you are still in your sins." (1 Corinthians 15:16-23) The afterlife and continuation of soul is a lynchpin of Paul's thought.

Furthermore, the resurrection is a result of God's love for humanity and a reward for following the correct path. "For God did not send his Son into the world to condemn the world, but in order that the world might be saved through him." (John 3:17)

For Muslims the existence of the soul is revealed in the **QUR'AN** and supported by the **HADITH**. The soul according to Muhammad is formed in the womb. According to Muslim scholars, who were influenced by **ARISTOTLE**, that soul is what gives the body life. The soul contains the **WILL** of a person. **PERSONAL IDENTITY** is defined by the choices of the soul. On Judgement Day the soul is judged by Allah based on those choices and attains eternal life through Allah's grace. Positive judgement means eternal life in paradise, whilst sinners will suffer in Jahannam (hell). "And to every soul will be paid in full (the fruit) of its deeds; and Allah knoweth best all that they do." (Surah 39:70)

For Muslims, Muhammad's **NIGHT JOURNEY** is further proof of the afterlife. In this journey Muhammad ascends to heaven, meets the Prophets and receives guidance from Allah. This is described as a physical as well as spiritual experience for Muhammad.

Finally, argue for life after death on the basis of fairness: that because there is unfairness in this world, there must be a world beyond where the imbalance is addressed. Kant believed that acting morally was a **DUTY** and the logical conclusion of practical reason or thought. We are all aiming towards supreme goodness or the **SUMMUM BONUM**. This is not possible in this world because bad things happen to good people. He writes: "The summum bonum, then, practically is only possible on the supposition of the immortality of the soul." Kant claims that this belief is beyond the boundaries of proof and is only the logical conclusion of moral reasoning.

Strengths

- **EXPLAINS HUMAN EXPERIENCE** - Monism (no division between mind and body) requires that human experience is reduced to the interaction of cells in the brain. This does not match the personal experience of **PERSONAL IDENTITY** and the "I". Dualism provides a way for that personal experience to be explains and preserved.

- **HOPE** - The inevitability of death is terrifying for many people. This only gets worse as people get older or become sick. Dualism, through the separation of the mind and the body, allows for a person to survive death. This provides hope for them that death is not the end, their good actions will be rewarded in the afterlife and they can see their loved ones that have passed away.

Weaknesses

- **LACK OF PROOF** - Dualism has a lack of testable scientific proof. Neither the "world of the forms" nor the Cartesian immaterial soul are made of the same substance as our reality, therefore the same rules of measurement and detection do not apply. Without proof it is more likely that the soul does not exist.

- **ISSUES OF INTERACTION** - Neither Plato nor Descartes is able to explain the exact relationship between the body and the soul. Descartes offered the **PINEAL GLAND** as the "principal seat of the soul" but this was disproved as neuroscience developed. Despite this suggestion, in reality it seems impossible that two metaphysically unique substances which share no similar qualities can interact. Even if the soul did exist, Descartes' belief that it controlled the body seems impossible.

MATERIALISM

Materialism is the belief that the soul and the body are not separate entities. There are two types of materialist: **SOFT** and **HARD**. Hard materialists believe that the qualities that are attributed to the soul are **REDUCIBLE** to physical activities of the body and the brain. Soft materialists believe that there are some qualities, such as consciousness, that are irreducible. There is nothing independent and the body and mind are interconnected. Both forms of materialism believe that when the body dies so does the mind. The "I" is not distinct from the body.

Gilbert Ryle

Gilbert Ryle, a hard materialist, stated that viewing the soul as "the ghost in the machine" which controls the body and is able to leave after the body has died is mistaken. This "category mistake" occurs when people talk about the body and the soul as different phenomena. The qualities of the mind are reducible to the actions of the body. Believing that the soul exists separate to the body would be like believing that "team spirit" exists separate from the players involved. The "soul" of a person is nothing more than their personal qualities and beliefs. When you talk about a person's soul you are only describing the things that they do, say or act like. It is not something separate and unique.

Richard Dawkins

Dawkins is another hard materialist, and he also rejects the idea of a separate soul. Human qualities are reducible entirely to their DNA and the influence of their environment. He believes that the concept of a soul implies a creator God. Evolution through natural selection explains the existence of life on Earth without need for reference to God. Importantly, although the qualities of consciousness that we experience as humans are reducible to bodily processes this does not devalue them. The fact that humans exist against all odds of chance is more amazing than the idea of a creator God. Humans should not worry about fulfilment in the next life. Instead they should focus their attention on the now. This will make them better humans and the world a better place.

John Hick

Hick, a soft materialist, argued that although the soul and the body are indivisible it is still "logically possible" that life after death could exist. We would be able to survive death if God created an identical "replica" of us in the afterlife. He is able to do this because He is omnipotent. **HICK** used a thought experiment to show that we can prove this "replica" is continuous with us and has the same **PERSONAL IDENTITY**. Importantly, **HICK'S** use of "replica" asserts that only one copy of the individual exists at the same time.

Imagine a person who disappears suddenly in New York, and an exact "replica" reappears in London. After studying this person we would eventually conclude that it was the same person. Importantly, he has not moved through time and space. He has disappeared and reappeared in a different location. Now, imagine that instead of disappearing in New York he dies. Following his death a "replica" reappears in London. Even if we had the body **HICK** argues that we would eventually conclude it was the same person. Finally, imagine after dying a "replica" appears in another world, a resurrection world inhabited by resurrected "replicas". Hick claims the "replica" would still be considered the same person because it would have the "sameness" as the original individual.

HICK converted to Christianity following a religious experience. His **REPLICA THEORY** is consistent with **PAUL'S** teaching regarding the resurrection of the body after death. **PAUL** taught that deserving and just humans would be resurrected by God like Jesus. He writes: "He who raised Christ Jesus from the dead will also give life to your mortal bodies through his Spirit who dwells in you." (Romans 8:11) Humans will be resurrected with a **SPIRITUAL** body in the afterlife. The physical body is left behind, enabling them to evolve through eternal life. He writes: "But someone will ask, 'How are the dead raised? With what kind of body do they come?' You foolish person! What you sow does not come to life unless it dies." (1 Corinthians 15:35)

PAUL knew that the physical body would not survive death. As the Bible states, "by the sweat of your brow you will eat your food until you return to the ground, since from it you were taken; for dust you are and to dust you will return". (Genesis 3:19) But he believed that people would be **RESURRECTED** like Jesus.

When Jesus was resurrected the disciples did not believe that he was real. He said: "Look at my hands and my feet. It is I myself! Touch me and see; a ghost does not have flesh and bones, as you see I have." (Luke 24:39) Jesus had a physical body; however, there was a difference from his pre-resurrection body, as he wasn't recognisable until he made himself known. "If there is a natural body, there is also a spiritual body." (1 Corinthians 15:44)

PAUL believed that the dead body will remain in the ground. This is because "flesh and blood cannot inherit the kingdom of God, nor does the perishable inherit the imperishable. Listen, I tell you a mystery: We will not all sleep, but we will all be changed." (1 Corinthians 15:50-51)

Like Jesus there would be a difference between the "physical body" that dies and the "spiritual body" that survives death. "There are also heavenly bodies and there are earthly bodies; but the splendour of the heavenly bodies is one kind, and the splendour of the earthly bodies is another." (1 Corinthians 15:40)

The resurrection is made possible because God is **OMNIPOTENT** and He changes the body so that it is able to overcome death and live forever: "For the perishable must clothe itself with the imperishable, and the mortal with immortality. When the perishable has been clothed with the imperishable, and the mortal with immortality, then the saying that is written will come true: 'Death has been swallowed up in victory.'" (1 Corinthians 15:53-54) The resurrected body is a spiritual body that is different from the earthly body.

Paul's view can be interpreted as a **SOFT MATERIALIST** position because he is not arguing for a separation of soul and body. Some elements of the body are retained in the afterlife.

PERSONAL POST-MORTEM EXPERIENCE

The Western interpretation of body and soul, influenced by the Judaeo-Christian tradition, claims that the "sameness" of a person continues after death. This "life" is a continuation of self following death. Many philosophers believe that this idea of **PERSONAL POST-MORTEM EXISTENCE** is impossible.

The dualist **JOHN LOCKE** believed that memory alone was sufficient for continuation of personal identity. "A thinking intelligent being, that has reason and reflection, and can consider itself as itself, the same thinking thing, in different times and places." As long as the memory extends "to any past action or thought, so far reaches the identity of that person; it is the same self now as it was then; and it is by the same self with this present one that now reflects on it, that that action was done". If after death the soul continues to remember the previous life then that soul is continuous with that life irrespective of the physical body.

BERNARD WILLIAMS claimed that this was inconsistent because memories are unreliable. Additionally, self definition is created as a response to the physical body. Beliefs such as "I am tall", "I am a man" or "I am good-looking" rely on physicality. Other fundamental attitudes a person might hold about, say, equality, fairness and justice are influenced by ethnicity, sexual orientation or physical disability. The personality is constructed as a response to the physical world it exists in. Even if there was a spiritual continuation of life after death without the physical characteristics to reinforce the beliefs, what continues could no longer be considered the same person.

MATERIALISTS also struggle against this challenge. Many beliefs are time-dependent. My choices now are affected by my view of myself in the future. My personality evolves and changes throughout time. Without time, my goals and ambitions would be meaningless and it seems hard to show how there can be a true continuation of self.

Conclusions

The issue of proof is the biggest challenge for those who believe that the soul is distinct from the body. The Judaeo-Christian and Islamic traditions rely on faith to overcome this issue but even with that they struggle to explain how **PERSONAL IDENTITY** can exist eternally without a physical body to give it meaning.

EASTERN RELIGIOUS INTERPRETATIONS

Key terms

- **ATMAN** - Hindu concept of soul.

- **ENLIGHTENMENT** - The highest state of man, where a human is free from the effects of desire.

- **INCARNATE** - Embodiment of a spirit in a physical form or body.

- **KARMA** - The law of cause and effect that governs rebirth and resurrection based on the intent and actions of an individual.

- **REBIRTH** - The belief that after death a life is reborn but is not identical to the life previous.

- **REINCARNATION** - The belief that after death the soul is reborn in a new body or new form

- **MOKSHA** - Liberation from the cycle of samsara.

- **SAMSARA** - The continual cycle of birth, death and rebirth.

The **DHARMIC** traditions struggle less with the concept of **PERSONAL POST-MORTEM EXISTENCE**. For Hindus the eternal soul that continues is not fixed. Instead it is on an eternal journey of continual change. An individual soul is likely to have existed for many lives previous, and the afterlife is the continuation of this cycle of **REINCARNATION** and **REBIRTH** called the wheel of **SAMSARA**.

When a person dies they are reincarnated into another life form. This is governed by the law of **KARMA**, which controls the outcome of the new life. Good moral actions produce positive karma, ensuring a positive rebirth whilst negative actions produce a negative rebirth. Karma differs from **FATE** because the actions of the soul whilst it is **INCARNATE** in a body impacts on the next life. This cycle of **SAMSARA** continues eternally until the soul or **ATMAN** attains **MOKSHA** (liberation from Samsara). This requires that the individual accepts the soul's oneness with the ultimate reality, or **BRAHMAN**, by removing desire and want.

Hindus believe in an eternal soul that continues after death. The soul is incarnated into a life and is reborn into a new life following the death of the original life form. Contrary to the Western view of the afterlife, the cycle of **SAMSARA** is a negative experience; a trap caused by attachment to material possessions and human relationships. When liberated the soul, or **ATMAN**, merges with **BRAHMAN** and the self disappears.

BUDDHISTS believe that the idea of a continuous soul or self is a myth. The Buddha claimed that the self is an illusion created as a result of attachment to worldly possessions and desires of the mind. We believe that we are continuous. This desire holds a person to the cycle of **SAMSARA**. Instead we should accept **ANATMAN** or "no-self", so we can attain **MOKSHA** (liberation) and overcome Samsara - which for Buddhists is a position of suffering. Through Moksha we achieve **NIRVANA** or **ENLIGHTENMENT** (which should not be confused with **HEAVEN**; it is not a place). Nirvana means "to extinguish". As desire is removed, Anatman is achieved and the illusion of self dissolves. The Buddha never fully explained what Nirvana was like but it is thought to be beyond human understanding.

Importantly, Buddhists differentiate between **REINCARNATION** and **REBIRTH**. They believe that the concept of reincarnation implies a continuous soul that lives after death. For example, if you were to die and be reincarnated as a cat, this would require an immortal soul that continues after your death. Buddhists do not believe in a soul that continues; it is more like a transferred flame. When a flame is transferred from one candle to the next there is a connection between the two, but they are different. Buddhist **REBIRTH** acknowledges the continuity between one life and the next but reinforces that the two are distinct. There is no personal post-mortem continuation.

NEAR-DEATH EXPERIENCES (NDEs)

As medical technology has developed, the line between death and living has blurred. It is now possible to bring people back from the brink of death through **RESUSCITATION** and **LIFE SUPPORT TECHNOLOGY**. In the 20th and 21st C people who have been brought back from the edge of death have reported strange out-of-body or communion-with-the-dead experiences. This phenomenon of the near-death experience (NDE) has been claimed by many to be the evidence that the theists have been seeking of an afterlife, and proof that the body and soul are distinct.

The psychologist **DR RAYMOND MOODY** coined the phrase **NEAR-DEATH EXPERIENCE** (NDE) in his book Life After Life while investigating the similarities between experiences people had reported after they had been brought back from the brink of death.

According to **MOODY**, people experiencing NDE claimed:
- they could hear a strange sound or ringing
- they felt at peace and were without pain
- they had an out-of-body experience where they floated above their body
- they witnessed a tunnel of light
- they rose rapidly through the sky and visited heaven
- they saw people shrouded in light, who were often loved ones
- they saw a "being" of goodness and light which they associated with Jesus and God
- they saw their life flash before their eyes and they could review their life
- they did not want to return, but after speaking to their loved ones or the being of light they were told it was not their "time" to die.

For **MOODY** the most profound feature of NDE for the people he interviewed was their experience with the "**BEING OF LIGHT**". Moody's research showed that the identification of this "being" depending on the religious background of the individual. Those of Christian faith or upbringing associated it with Christ, while Jewish individuals have described it as an angel. Those without faith talked of it being a guide. To most the **BEING OF LIGHT** had no physical body - it was only light - but to the individual it was a personal being. In many experiences the **BEING OF LIGHT** communicated with them in an unknown language that they were able to understand, and asked them life-reviewing questions such as "what have you done with your life?" and "are you prepared to die?".

To **MOODY** the **CERTAINTY** and **UNIFORMITY** of experience is evidence that there is an afterlife. He writes: "I have absolutely no fear of death. From my near-death research and my personal experiences, death is, in my judgement, simply a transition into another kind of reality."

PMH ATWATER experienced three NDEs in 1977. Following her personal NDE experiences and others she has studied, she provides five insights into the phenomenon.

The first is that NDE tell us "what it feels like to die". There is a lack of pain and a recognition that physical death does not end life. Most people feel "more alive" during their death than normal. The second is that whilst dying you "shift your field of reality", analogous to the changing of a radio station. These frequencies of life exist in parallel to each other and death moves you into a different understanding. Thirdly, "existence is more than time and space". Time and space are elements of the physical world and do not exist beyond it. Through NDE people can experience the reality of existence as eternal and neverending. Fourthly,

"God is real but is not a physical being". The terms we use are just ways to describe the relationship between humans and God. Fifthly, through NDE we can understand the "big picture" - that God is not judgement, but love.

Atwater categorises four different types of NDE from her study of adults and children.

- Initial experience or non-experience - In these experiences people experience "nothingness". Crucially, that nothingness is not threatening but is loving or friendly. This may be coupled with an out-of-body experience or the engagement with a friendly voice.

- Unpleasant experience - Sometimes called hell-like experiences, during these experiences people report that they have visited a "hell" zone, with possible "hauntings" from the persons passed, or they experience a threatening void/nothingness. These are less reported.

- Pleasant or heaven-like experience - These are typified by reunion with loved ones who have died or the meeting of significant religious figures such as Jesus. They often include reassuring conversations about the person's life.

- Transcendent experience - These experiences take the observer beyond their usual frame of reference. They often include significant revelations of truth and are mostly non-personal.

Interestingly, each category is typified by a psychological **PREDISPOSITION** of the person experiencing. For example; pleasant/ heaven experiences are mostly observed by people who have a desire to be loved and have a strong belief in fate, while hell experiences are related to those with repressed issues or a strong sense of guilt. Often, after going through any of these experiences people have a **CHANGE** in their attitude. The experience gives them a perspective on life that can help shape it in the future.

For **ATWATER**, NDEs can contain elements of each category and their uniformity is not complete, but the certainty of the witnesses and her own experience are proof of the afterlife.

DR KENNETH RING, inspired by **MOODY**, attempted a more scientific investigation into NDEs. He interviewed 102 people covering a variety of ages, backgrounds and afflictions, including blind people, suicide attempters, theists and atheists. He found that people reported very similar experiences to those of **MOODY** and **ATWATER**: light, out-of-body experiences, joy, loved ones etc. He concluded that NDEs are not hallucinations because they are very lucid and create concrete memories, unlike hallucinations. Additionally, religious faith has no influence on the depth or intensity of the experience, as atheists and theists reported similar experiences. NDEs also affect people regardless of social class, race, age, gender, education or marital status, and most are left with a profound new understanding of life and a transformation in attitudes and values.

What qualifies an experience as **NDE** has been debated by many. Psychiatrist **BRUCE GREYSON** developed his **GREYSON SCALE** to measure the **DEPTH** of an individual's near-death experience and separate NDEs from psychological disorders. He formulated it based upon interviews with 74 people who claimed to have had NDEs. The scale evaluates the intensity of 16 common features of NDEs, including experiencing altered time and reality, review of life, feeling of peace and joy, cosmic oneness, visions, experience of light, out-of-body experience, communion with dead or religious figures, and a border or point of no return. He says, "A typical near-death experience occurs when someone is on the threshold of death or has actually been pronounced dead."

One case **GREYSON** reports is of nine-year-old Eddie Cuomo, who was suffering an intense fever for 36 hours. When the fever broke at 3am he reported that he had spoken to his deceased grandfather and his teenage sister Teresa. The family had spoken to their daughter two days previously; she was studying in Vermont. Later on that day they discovered that Teresa had died around 12am in a car accident at roughly the same time that Eddie was in his fevered state.

GREYSON used his scale with the same group of people 20 years later to evaluate the reliability of their evidence. He believed that false accounts would become embellished over time. Interestingly, his results showed that the average score of people on his scale remained constant. The lack of embellishment shows that reporting of **NDE**s is **RELIABLE**.

Scientific explanations for NDEs

Despite the application of scientific method to their research, the conclusions of Moody, Atwater, Ring, Greyson and other NDE supporters are held to represent a **MINORITY** position. Many scientists have sought to disprove the mystical element of NDE, and provide a psychological or physiological explanation for the phenomenon.

THE DYING BRAIN - For NDE theorists the consistency of experience between individuals is proof that NDEs are real. **SUSAN BLACKMORE** challenges this assumption. She says that the "sameness" experienced by people is not spiritual but a feature of the **DYING BRAIN**. Because all human brains are very similar when they die they will present similar responses, especially when they are put under the same stress. This is why NDEs feature the same core experiences.

HALLUCINATION - Current research into hallucinogenic drugs shows that instead of heightening awareness they reduce blood flow to areas of the brain concerned with perception. The reduced oxygen blurs human perception and causes hallucinations. When the brain dies this effect is replicated; as oxygen and blood levels fall in crucial perception zones the brain begins to hallucinate and this effect has been misreported as NDE. **DR RONALD SIEGEL** claims that with the right circumstances he has been able to recreate drug-induced hallucinations that resemble NDEs in some of his volunteers. This he believes is proof that NDEs are nothing more than vivid hallucinations.

NO MEDICAL DANGER - Scientists **DEAN MOBBS** and **CAROLINE WATT** believe that there are explanations for NDE. They claim that in 50 per cent of the NDEs they studied, the person reporting was not actually in danger of dying. In some cases, the fear of **DEATH** is what produces an NDE. The **CULTURAL AWARENESS** of NDE may produce a "self fulfilling prophecy" to explain the unusual sensations a person has experienced.

Moreover, the experiences of NDE are not exclusive. "Walking Corpse" or Cotard syndrome produces a delusion that the person is deceased. Often associated with trauma and linked to the parietal cortex, it is believed that Cotard's syndrome is a mental response to help understand the strange experiences a person is going through.

HYPERAWARENESS - Recent studies on rats suggest that at the point of death there is a peak of brain activity. **DR JIMO BORJIGIN** suggests that as the brain dies it does not shut down, but instead it is more active than when it is awake. This defence mechanism and resultant **HYPERAWARENESS** caused by a surge of electrical activity could result in vivid experiences associated with NDE.

Conclusion

Estimates put the reports of NDE at between 40 and 60 per cent of hose who approach the brink of death. The cases studied show an interesting correlation of experience, with most reporting very similar experiences of peace, joy, love and also visits from religious or spiritual figures. This consistency, reports of new knowledge and the life-transforming impact of NDE for some are the only evidence needed to prove the existence of NDE and the afterlife. However, many scientists question this notion of proof, claiming that it is just a symptom of the process of death and the more we learn about what the brain goes through as it dies the more we will be able to explain the phenomenon. Whatever the truth is, this debate will continue, fuelled by the strange experiences of people who come close to death.

Issues arising

- Is the notion of personal post-mortem existence coherent?

- Do near-death experiences provide reasonable grounds for belief in the afterlife?

- Is the notion of soul coherent, and are there reasonable grounds for belief in the existence of a soul?

Key quotes

1. *"Ordinary people seem not to realise that those who really apply themselves in the proper way to philosophy are directly and of their own accord preparing themselves for death and dying."* Plato

2. *"All you may know of heaven or hell is within your own self."* Edgar Cayce

3. *"Then the Lord God formed the man of dust from the ground and breathed into his nostrils the breath of life, and the man became a living creature."* Genesis 2:7

4. *"The end of life is to be like God, and the soul following God will be like Him."* Socrates

5. *"For the perishable must clothe itself with the imperishable, and the mortal with immortality. When the perishable has been clothed with the imperishable, and the mortal with immortality, then the saying that is written will come true: 'Death has been swallowed up in victory.'"* 1 Corinthians 15:53-54

Confusions to avoid

Do not ignore the relationship of the soul to the body. A common mistake is to focus on the nature of the soul and to ignore the issue of interaction. **DUALISM** needs a coherent explanation of the interaction between the soul and the body if it is to survive the critics. When revising each topic, make notes regarding how the two interact and what the implications of that interaction are. **DESCARTES'** focus on the pineal gland implies that there is a specific point of interaction. Some claim that his view is inconsistent. On order to interact the soul must have extension in space. This is a feature of the physical world. For **PLATO** the interaction is negative. The soul or true reality of a person is clouded by the body. Its ignorance prevents it remembering knowledge and inhibits spiritual progression. Understanding the nature of this interaction and being able to criticise these assertions is a crucial part of the specification.

Develop an understanding of what constitutes the "I" and the relationship between "I" and the body. For each theory, examine how an individual could survive in the new state. Could a person's thoughts, memories and beliefs exist without a body? Furthermore, would a change in the nature of that person affect the continuation of that life in the afterlife? Near-death experience does not avoid the challenge of personal post-mortem existence, and should also be evaluated in light of this.

John Hick thought experiment was a proof of the **LOGICAL POSSIBILITY** of resurrection. He does not state that this is physical proof. Hick's replica theory is a thought experiment to show how it would be possible for God to resurrect humans and demonstrate that with omnipotence that this would be possible.

When discussing NDE, give specific examples. This will give the features such as feelings of awe, feelings of peace and experiences of light context. This will provide a more developed answer than simply listing the features.

GET MORE HELP

Get more help with body, soul and personal identity by using the links below:

http://i-pu.sh/Z1W02H50

The Problem of Evil

Key terms

- **EPISTEMIC DISTANCE** - Distance from knowledge of God.

- **ESCHATOLOGICAL** - Normally referring to the end times, or the end of history; in Hick's theory it refers to post-death.

- **MORAL EVIL** - Intentional actions by humans which cause suffering.

- **NATURAL EVIL** - Events in nature which result in suffering.

- **OMNIBENEVOLENT** - Literally "all good"; God, a being who is all good or loving.

- **OMNIPOTENT** - Literally "all power"; God having the characteristic of being all-powerful.

- **OMNISCIENT** - Literally "all knowledge"; God knowing all things, including future events.

- **PRIVATIO BONI** - The privation of good; evil is not a substance or entity but the privation, or lack, of good.

Please support our learning community by not photocopying without a licence

- **THEODICY** - Literally, theos (God), diké (justice); an attempt to justify the existence of God in the face of the existence of evil and suffering. In particular the attempt to defend the existence of a God with the attributes of omnipotence and omnibenevolence.

WHAT DO WE MEAN BY EVIL?

Scholars have classically divided evil into two types, though in reality there are many links between these types and the distinction between the two is not always easy to delineate (for example, think about an event such as a flood following heavy rain; this would seem like a natural event, but might actually have been caused, or made much worse, by deforestation carried out by man). The two types are:

- **MORAL EVIL** - This term is used to denote evil actions committed by human beings, such as rape, murder and war, as well as actions which result in psychological and mental pain. These actions are freely committed and result in suffering, sometimes on a mass scale. There are countless accounts of atrocities that show the depth of human cruelty, including modern-day examples.

- **NATURAL EVIL** - Events in nature that cause suffering, and which are not directly the result of human action, such as earthquakes and hurricanes. Disease and illness would also come under the title of natural evil. Philosophers disagree as to whether such "natural" events should be called "evil".

THE PROBLEM

- If God is all-good he would not allow moral and natural evil to exist. Having a **BENEVOLENT** nature, he would have the motivation to abolish evil.

- If God was all-powerful, he would be able to stop evil. Having an **OMNIPOTENT** nature, he would have the ability to eliminate it entirely.

- And yet **EVIL EXISTS**.

Within the Judaeo-Christian tradition, God is also believed to be **OMNISCIENT** (although this is often included as an element of omnipotence). Omniscience raises further issues because it would imply that God knows that evil is going to happen but does not prevent it from doing so. The nature of God as the **CREATOR** is also relevant here; if God created everything in the universe ex nihilo then the question needs to be asked if God created evil.

Earlier arguments concerning whether the universe has an ultimate purpose and meaning also come into play. A **THEODICY** attempts to reach a "big picture" conclusion about why things exist (including the possibility of a "purpose" for the existence of evil), whereas many think such a search for overarching reason and meaning is both futile and unnecessary. Indeed, Russell finds the idea of the world as accident more plausible than the world as a **PURPOSEFUL** work of a God.

On the evidence of the immense amount of suffering in the world, Russell states that the most fitting description of God, if he existed, would be "a fiend".

A key question is: how can an all-loving and all-powerful God tolerate one incident of suffering in his creation? Is there a solution to this problem which maintains God's character as understood in classical theism even in the face of evil or, as **HUME** suggests, does one of these attributes of God have to be removed to solve the inconsistency?

The attempt to justify the existence of God in the face of evil and suffering is called a **THEODICY**. Whilst some scholars such as **RUBENSTEIN** say that it is impossible to frame a theodicy after the horrors of Auschwitz, those that are formulated normally attempt to:

- blame a source other than God for the existence of evil, or

- say why evil is justified or even necessary for a greater good, or

- reinterpret (without removing) what is meant by omnibenevolence and omnipotence.

Few theodicies take the line that evil does not exist (they cease to be theodicies if they do), but **AUGUSTINE** does conclude that evil is not a substance as such, as explained below.

THE THEODICY OF AUGUSTINE

AUGUSTINE'S THEODICY continues to have influence upon Christian thought, 15 centuries after it was written. We can take his argument step by step:

Augustine's opening premise was that God, who is perfect, and therefore all-powerful and all-loving, made a good world. He based this understanding on the teaching of **GENESIS**, where God declared that his creation was good at the end of each of the first five days and very good at the end of the sixth. The universe, with a **HIERARCHY OF**

BEINGS from God down to angels, humans and the rest of creation, was ordered and in harmony.

However, after the creation of a good universe, both angels and man fell. The **FALL OF ADAM AND EVE** is outlined in Genesis chapter 3. Augustine argued that they clearly **FREELY CHOSE TO DISOBEY GOD**. They chose not to do what is good and rejected what God had told them to do and in so doing chose "non-being" material things rather than the fullness of their being, God. Hence, by their **ORIGINAL SIN** of disobedience to God's instructions, Adam and Eve introduced a break and discord between them and their creator, God. Humanity **FELL** from a close relationship with God.

This "choosing" of evil" was actually choosing to not live up to the standard of goodness that God intended; because it was choosing not to do that which is good, it is a **PRIVATION**. By this, Augustine meant that **EVIL IS THE LACK OF GOODNESS**, as blindness is the lack of sight. To stress, evil, in Augustine's theodicy, is not a **SUBSTANCE**, but the lack of good. In Latin, the phrase is **PRIVATIO BONI**. We can think about this idea of privation using many examples - cold is the absence of heat, ill-health the absence of health, etc - and these things only have understanding in relation to what they lack. Adam and Eve now lack "right order" and harmony with God - they have chosen to be **DEPRIVED**.

The idea of "**LACK**" is very important, but be careful. It is not evil that a stone lacks the ability to talk, or a worm lacks the ability to walk. These are qualities that the stone and the worm lack, but because they lack them they are not evil. However, when man chooses to not "hit the mark" (this is what "to sin" means), he is evil in the sense that he fails to live up to his morally good and God-given nature. And the choice to do this is due to our **FREE WILL**, and hence carries with it

RESPONSIBILITY. If someone cannot use their arm due to an accident, they lack the health of the arm, but they cannot help this, unlike the lack of kindness we show when we are cruel to someone. On this point **TAYLOR** writes:

> *"According to Augustine's view, if you say that a human being is evil, or that their actions are evil, you are saying that the way they behave does not match expectations about how a human being should behave."*

Evil therefore comes about because of Adam and Eve's **FREE MORAL CHOICE**. Adam and Eve, when tempted by **LUCIFER**, use their free will to not live to the standards for which they were created, and through this disobedience evil enters the world; as noted, evil here is not as a substance in itself, but the lack of goodness. Both moral and natural evil stem from the wrong moral choices made. Pain in childbirth and hard work making the soil productive are both immediate results listed in **GENESIS 3**. **MORAL EVIL** comes through Adam and Eve's choice, which sets them at a distance from God; **NATURAL EVIL** is due to the balance of nature being upset and the work of the fallen angel **LUCIFER**, who tries to be more powerful than God, bringing discord to nature which results in suffering. But **AUGUSTINE** argued that free will is a good thing in itself, as it enables good and right choices to be made and is worth the price of evil occurring. Of course, if God is perfect, he would have known humanity would make a wrong choice and fall, but he chose for humans to have free will so that they could freely love him rather than be robots without choice.

AUGUSTINE argued that the goodness of the world is seen clearly when people choose to do good, as it stands in contrast to when people do evil and misuse their free will, just as "a dash of black makes the colours in a painting stand out". (**PHELAN**) This is known as the **AESTHETIC PRINCIPLE**, as Augustine writes:

> *"In the universe, even that which is called evil, when it is regulated and put in its own place, only enhances our admiration of the good; for we enjoy and value the good more when we compare it with the evil."*

God did not create anything **IMPERFECT**; he could not therefore have created evil. Thus, evil is not a "thing". Neither is God in a **BATTLE** between the forces of good and evil - spiritual forces at war might make people not responsible for their choices, and **AUGUSTINE** stressed that human responsibility stemmed from humans being free to choose. But be careful not to say that Augustine denied that evil existed; it "exists" not as a separate "thing", because God would have had to have made it if it was a thing, but as a **LACK OF GOODNESS**. Indeed, later Augustine goes on to say that evil comes from God due to the fact that he keeps human beings in existence, and they are beings who have this free choice to become evil.

Now Augustine has established that Adam and Eve's choice gives birth to evil, how does he account for ongoing evil in the world? As all humanity is descended from Adam and Eve, then all humans inherit their **SINFUL NATURE**, which chooses to live in rebellion towards, and in discord with, God, and not reach the standard for which God created us. Augustine says that humans are "**SEMINALLY PRESENT**" in Adam, and, as such, our punishment is deserved.

For Augustine, "all evil is either sin or punishment for sin".

However, Christ is the "**SECOND ADAM**" who shows God's grace and mercy in offering humanity a chance to restore its relationship with God and avert hell, which would be just punishment for sin.

Key steps:

1. Creation is perfect; God is all-powerful and all-loving.

2. Adam and Eve have free choice - a good thing.

3. They, and Satan, freely chose not to do good - **PRIVATIO BONI** (the Fall). God does not create evil.

4. Humans and angels are responsible for this choice, which brings moral and natural evil into the world, resulting in suffering.

5. The goodness in the world as a whole can clearly be seen when contrasted with when people choose the privatio boni. God keeps in existence people who have freedom to choose not to be good.

6. The sinful nature of Adam is present in humans.

7. Jesus offers a way for human nature to be restored.

Strengths

- **INHERENT GOODNESS** - It could be argued that the default position of humanity is good, in that we are offended when people do harm; news reports are full of things which go against our expectations, such as murder and conflict, and this is why they are news. Is this a hint that the world is "good", as Augustine suggested, and that evil is a privation of that goodness?

- The idea of **EVIL LACKING SUBSTANCE** can make **LOGICAL SENSE**, just as darkness being the absence of light and cold the absence of heat are logically coherent ideas. **LAW** has recently challenged this idea, however, and said that from the clues in the universe, God might in fact be evil; such a God just puts some good in the world to let people think he is good. He argues that the idea that "God is evil" can be supported from the world with as much credence as the idea that "God is good".

- If **FREEDOM AND RESPONSIBILITY** are to be genuine, then our choices have to have consequences, otherwise it does not matter what we choose to do. It has been argued that this is the type of freedom we seem to experience and which is at the heart of **AUGUSTINE'S THEODICY**. The alternative to unrestricted moral freedom seems to suggest something less than what it means to be human.

Weaknesses

- **EXPERIENCE** may agree with the idea that evil is simply the lack of good? To those who have been victims of rape or violence, or genocide on a mass scale, there seems to be more than the **PRIVATIO BONI** at work. It does not seem that the careful planning, organisation and implementation of shockingly cruel and depraved acts which were part of the Holocaust can be explained by thousands of people just lacking the good.

- **REASONS** - Does Augustine's theory explain **WHY** angels and humans should choose to not obey God? It would seem that this even stumped Augustine; concerning why the will should be turned not to do the right thing, he said "let no one seek to know from me what I know that I do not know".

- **ILLOGICAL** - God's goodness can be questioned if the whole system is set up in a way that allows for such suffering on a massive scale. Schleiermacher has pointed out the **LOGICAL CONTRADICTION** in the idea that a perfect world could go wrong. And how could such a world go wrong if there was no knowledge of evil for humanity to choose at the Fall?

- **SUFFERING** - **DOSTOYEVSKY** questioned the idea of a loving God based on the sheer amount of suffering in the world, even if it allows humans to be free; is God's loving gift of freedom worth this cost? It would be difficult to quantify how much suffering is too much; should toothache not be allowed, for example? Others have questioned how a good God could conceive of the existence of a punishment such as **HELL**.

THE THEODICY OF IRENAEUS

While Augustine's theodicy is sometimes called a **SOUL-DECIDING THEODICY**, as we choose/decide what we will do with the good gift of free will, **IRENAEUS'** argument is known as a **SOUL-MAKING THEODICY**. It has within it a very different idea of the source of evil. Writing 200 years before Augustine, Irenaeus' theodicy works in the following way:

- Irenaeus read the **GENESIS** creation account **LITERALLY**. From this basis he argued that God desires for humanity to reach **PERFECTION**, but that this perfection is something to be reached from an initial state of imperfection (this is different to Augustine's belief of humans falling away from perfection). Humans are created **IMMATURE**, but can progress towards maturity and perfection. Irenaeus worked with the teaching of

GENESIS 1 verse 26, where humans were made in the "**IMAGE**" of God, but were to develop into the "**LIKENESS**" of God.

- It is important to unpack this idea. **COLE** notes that this is a move from the "form" (image) of God to the content (likeness) of God. The Good News translation of the Bible uses the words "they (people) will be like us (God) and resemble us." **TAYLOR** et al note that Irenaeus understands "like us" as God creating people with "intelligence, morality and a personality" and the state of "resembling" God as peoples' souls growing "until they resembled the very nature of God."

- Being child-like, humans make **MISTAKES** and do things which are not wise, but this is a result of both their lack of maturity and the **FREEDOM** they have. In Genesis chapter 3, Adam and Eve are exiled, (through an actual event known as the Fall), from the Garden of Eden to make the journey towards God's likeness in a world which is suited for them to make such a pilgrimage. Whilst they do bear some responsibility for their choices against God's commands, **IRENAEUS** held that the serpent who tricked them is to blame. Adam and Eve are banished from the garden, but this is not punishment in the Augustine sense; **TAYLOR** notes that such punishment is offered in the way children are set boundaries, and it is therefore "educative". Neither is the Fall as catastrophic for **IRENAEUS** as it is for **AUGUSTINE** as it is a mistake which is part of the human experience of growing up, rather than a movement away from perfection, and there certainly is no sense of "**ORIGINAL SIN**" in Irenaeus' theodicy, unlike there is in Augustine's.

- In the playground of this world, humanity can develop, and grow towards "good." Evil and suffering provide **TESTS** for that growth but humans can make moral progress in the world as they journey. Irenaeus noted that in the bible there were many people, such as **JONAH**, who went through suffering in order to grow, make mistakes, learn the need to repent and fulfil the purposes God had for them. How we react to this suffering is the key. And **JESUS**, through suffering, restores the damage that Adam has done by his choice and makes it possible for there to be union between God and man again. Jesus rescues those taken captive by the serpent by taking Adam's sin on the cross, restoring friendship between God and man.

Thus, **EVIL IS NECESSARY** as an essential part of the environment in which humanity can grow, in which we can choose to live above our basic animal instincts. God, who is all-good and all-powerful, allows evil and suffering as part of the environment in which the journey from imperfection to perfection takes place and therefore there is purpose for both good and evil within the creation of the universe. (This is very different to **AUGUSTINE**'s explanation of evil.) Evil and suffering are necessary in order to help us develop **MORAL VIRTUE** and maturity, to grow in character to resemble God, and be good like him, eventually achieving perfection. Without suffering and the prospect of death, there is no testing which provides opportunity for growth and repentance and learning of what is good; neither would there be any contrast between what is good and what is evil (see the aesthetic principle). For Irenaeus evil is not a privation, but a very real and necessary part of the world in which we develop towards maturity. As **AHLUWALIA** writes, "evil was necessarily for the existence of good". If so, does this offer a possible philosophical answer to the problem of evil?

Because the world is like this, it is what **HICK** calls, a "**VALE OF SOUL-MAKING**". Our souls can choose to live towards ourselves or towards God, to develop kindness and empathy and to learn from our mistakes. Being created perfect would not have given us the opportunity to develop and learn. This growth requires a determination of the will within the reality that the choices we make with our free will have consequences. Expecting to be bailed out every time we make an error would not develop our souls and would compromise genuine free will.

The journey **CONTINUES AFTER DEATH** because the soul carries on its journey until ready to enter heaven; it is important, however, to note that for Irenaeus those who continue to reject God and who do not grow will face punishment post-death.

HICK has developed Irenaeus' ideas to argue that humanity is able to make this evolutionary journey towards a relationship with God. He argues that in this world humanity is at an **EPISTEMIC DISTANCE** from God, meaning at a distance of knowing God, and can, through free choice, make a journey towards God, developing goodness in the face of a world which contains evil and disasters. The world seems to be one which is entirely suited to enable soul-making to go on. Indeed, our **RESPONSE** to catastrophic events can potentially help to **DEVELOP CHARACTER** traits such as empathy, kindness and compassion. Humans have the knowledge of the laws of nature in which they can explore the world, but it is precisely those predictable and regular **LAWS OF NATURE** which govern the fact that earthquakes and hurricanes exist, or bricks remain hard (and do not suddenly by some divine intervention become soft) when they fall on someone's head. In addition to this, because of the fact that we are truly free, we can cause suffering, or have pain inflicted on us. **HICK** argues that without the possibility of these dangers, **NO PROGRESS WOULD BE MADE** either within the soul of a person or in any area of life such as the arts or the sciences, and in a world of no suffering, nothing actually would ever be seen as right or wrong. No real virtues would develop when we act kindly without the possibility of us not choosing this path and acting maliciously.

Eventually everyone will be able to enter into a relationship with God post-death in a **UNIVERSAL ESCHATOLOGICAL SALVATION**.

THE FREE WILL DEFENCE

Central to the theodicies of **AUGUSTINE**, **IRENAEUS** and **HICK** is the idea that there has to be evil and suffering in the world if humans are to be genuinely free; we have to have **THE POSSIBILITY OF CHOOSING WRONG**, with the **REAL CONSEQUENCES** of those choices, in order for us to be **TRULY FREE**.

For Augustine, the choice made when humanity misused free will resulted in evil which is taken on the cross by Christ. For Irenaeus the free will to choose is part of our soul's development towards the likeness of God.

Is this freedom worth the cost? What are the alternatives? **MACKIE** suggests that God could have made a world in which humans always choose what is good, but many have rejected this as not what is meant by freedom. Others have suggested that perhaps our choices could result in less suffering than they seem to in this world. Others question whether a God of love should have made such a world at all.

Strengths

- Does part of what it means to be human and **GENUINELY FREE** necessarily involve the possibility of choosing good and evil? Irenaeus argued that for a person to have any less a choice would mean he is no longer human. What would it mean for human identity if freedom wasn't genuine and there weren't good and bad choices to be made?

- Could the development of humanity really have happened **WITHOUT RISK**, or danger or difficulty? Would virtuous choices develop if we did not have **ALTERNATIVE CHOICES** that we could make? Would we progress if God intervened all the time rather than letting us learn from our mistakes? Is it better and **MORE LOVING** parenting to set boundaries (laws of nature), but allow freedom within those boundaries and encourage (rather than dictate) good choices? Do we sometimes work on the principle that some suffering is indeed worth the end result? If so, is it possible to translate that principle to a cosmic level?

- **POST-DEATH** resolution of the problem of suffering might indeed be a way of fulfilling God's purpose for people to move from being in God's image to his likeness. It would suggest that for those who suffer unimaginable pain in this life, the whole journey is **NOT FUTILE**, which, if this life was all there was, it might seem to be. Is it possible to offer alternative hope if there is no life after death?

Weaknesses

- It is difficult to understand why there needs to be the **EXTREME AMOUNT** of suffering in the world for humans to learn. After a certain amount of pain, the human soul might actually fail to learn its lesson. For children born into extreme poverty, involving malnutrition, to suggest the idea of suffering as a soul-making journey could seem almost immoral. If, further to that, such children are to continue their journey of soul-making in the afterlife (what does this mean - that they would suffer further, post-death, in order to learn and develop more?), would this seem fair or loving in any way? In reference to this idea, suffering seems to be so randomly allocated.

- **PHILLIPS** questions how a **GOD OF LOVE** can **JUSTIFY SUFFERING** to fulfil his purposes. He is particularly critical of viewing a kind response to the suffering of others as a way of developing one's soul; it would almost suggest that people should look for the suffering of others and, in a way, be grateful for it as it gives them a chance to respond kindly and develop their character. Using suffering as a means to justify the end (**INSTRUMENTALISM**) of moral development is an example of a case where a theodicy adds to the problem of evil rather than solves it. Could there be alternative pain-free ways to develop the soul?

- How strong and philosophically valid is any theory that relies on post-death existence for its solution? Is the theodicy more likely to be accepted on **THEOLOGICAL** grounds by a believer than on **PHILOSOPHICAL** grounds by an atheist?

FURTHER CONSIDERATIONS

AUGUSTINE tried to move away from the idea of evil being "God's fault", whilst Irenaeus argued that evil could serve a purpose. In general, when writing about the "fault" idea, students should be careful. It could be useful to hold the "God's fault" argument in **BALANCE**. If God is blamed when an earthquake takes place, is it logical to thank him when one doesn't? If God is blamed for seemingly faulty features of the universe, is it consistent to thank him for beauty and laws of nature that mean, for example, trees grow and produce fruit? What would Augustine and **IRENAEUS** say about the "balance of blame and thanks"?

How does one classify illnesses such as cancer? If cancer occurs as a direct result of smoking, is **GOD** to be held **RESPONSIBLE** for the very possibility of the occurrence of cancer in the person, or is the smoker responsible for misusing their freedom, knowing the possible consequences? Could there be a world in which we could do what we like without bad side effects, or would this not be what we mean by human existence?

Is God's **OMNIPOTENCE** limited by logical possibilities, so that this type of world would be a logical contradiction, or, as **DESCARTES** argued, does God's omnipotence mean that he must be able to do anything and not be limited to what is logically possible? **BRAND** has written extensively on the idea that pain is God's gift to the world as without its use as a barrier on our actions, we would suffer even more. Further, he notes that the same sensitivity that withdraws fingers when placed on something sharp is precisely the same preciseness of touch needed to play the piano softly.

However, **HEBBLETHWAITE**, in **AHLUWALIA**, writes:

> "Part of the problem of evil is the fact that, the structure of
> our bodies, nerves and brains being what it is, physical and
> mental torture (as well as disease and accident) can take such
> horrific forms."

What would Augustine and Irenaeus say to these ideas?

Does God's foreknowledge of the Fall of Man and subsequent evil make
GOD ULTIMATELY RESPONSIBLE for it in Augustine's theodicy? Did
God not have the power to make humans not able to sin, if he could see
that we would? Augustine says:

> "God indeed had the power to make humans who could not
> sin. But He preferred to make them so that they had the
> power to sin or not sin as they wished. As a result there
> would be humans who gained merit from not sinning in this
> life and who received in the next the reward of not being able
> to sin." (See Saulitys)

Augustine seems to be saying that creating human beings able to sin is
not the same as "they will sin", and having free will and the possible
disastrous consequences of that is better than not having free will. But
does this still make God responsible if he knew humanity would choose
to use their free will for evil? Augustine responds by saying that humans
are not compelled to sin by external factors, just as a stone has no choice
but to fall when dropped. **MORAL EVIL**, unlike the stone's fall, is a
VOLUNTARY use of free will. Even though God's knowledge is perfect
and must include knowledge of the Fall of Man, humans freely make

choices. Augustine thinks God's omniscience and human freedom are compatible. Is this convincing?

Issues arising

- The success of the theodicies as a response to the problem of evil.

- What poses the greatest challenge to faith in God - natural or moral evil?

- Is free will a satisfactory explanation for the existence of evil in a world created by God?

- The strengths and weaknesses of these responses to the problem of evil.

Key quotes

1. *"Either God cannot abolish evil, or He will not; if He cannot, then He is not all-powerful; if He will not, then He is not all-good." Augustine*

2. *"According to Augustine there was no evil in creation before angelic and human sin. It came into existence when first angels, and then humans misused their wills turning from their creator." Saulytis*

3. *"God must have been on leave during the Holocaust."*
    Wiesenthal

4. *"God judged it better to bring good out of evil than to suffer*
    no evil to exist." Augustine

5. *"A world which is to be a person-making environment cannot*
    be a pain-free paradise but must contain challenges and
    dangers, with real possibilities of many kinds and disaster,
    and the pain and suffering which they bring." Hick

6. *"In a world devoid both of dangers to be avoided and*
    rewards to be won we may assume that there would have
    been virtually no moral development of the human intellect
    and imagination, and hence of either the sciences or the arts,
    and hence of human civilisation or culture." Hick

Confusions to avoid

- Note that the theodicies are put forward to defend the existence of a God who has certain characteristics. To simply say that the existence of evil in the world means it is impossible to believe in God is not what this topic is about. **ARISTOTLE'S PRIME MOVER**-type God has nothing to do with the world and therefore the existence of suffering would not at all be an argument against such a God, as the Prime Mover is never once declared as loving or interested in humanity. Be careful to note that theodicies are trying to justify why a **POWERFUL AND LOVING GOD** allows evil.

- Highlight the differences between **AUGUSTINE** and **IRENAEUS**, as their theodicies differ in many ways. Be very clear that you are aware of their explanations of the source of natural and moral evil, the role of free will, the purpose of evil and the ongoing effect of evil in the world. If you do use Hick's development of Irenaeus, make sure you say that that is what you are doing.

GET MORE HELP

Get more help with the problem of evil by using the links below:

http://i-pu.sh/S3F85S54

Exam Rescue Remedy

1. Build your own scaffolding which represents the logic of the theory. Use a mind map or a summary sheet.

2. Do an analysis of past questions by theme as well as by year (see philosophicalinvestigations.co.uk website for examples). Try writing your own Philosophy of Religion paper based on what hasn't come up recently.

3. Examine examiners' reports (go to their website) for clues as to how to answer a question well.

4. Use the **AREA** approach suggested in this revision guide. **ARGUMENT** - Have I explained the argument (from Plato or Kant for example)? **RESPONSE** - Have I outlined and explained a good range of responses to the argument? **EVALUATION** - Now I have clearly set out positions, what do I think of these? Is mine a **PHILOSOPHICAL** argument, and why? Does the original argument stand or fall against the criticisms raised? Why or why not?

5. List relevant technical vocabulary for inclusion in an essay (eg efficient cause, form of the good, analytic, synthetic).

6. Prepare key quotes from selected key authors, original/ contemporary - or even better, produce your own. Learn some.

7. Contrast and then evaluate different views/theories/authors, as some questions ask "which approach is best?" So contrast every approach with one other and decide beforehand what you think.

8. Practise writing for 35 minutes. Don't use a computer, unless you will do so in the exam.

9. Always answer and discuss the exact question in front of you,;never learn a "model answer". Use your own examples (newspapers, films, documentaries, real life). Be prepared to think creatively and adapt your knowledge to the question.

10. Conclude with your view, and justify it (give reasons) - especially with "discuss".

Bibliography

- **AHLUWALIA, L** - Understanding Philosophy of Religion OCR, Folens, 2008

- **BOWIE, R** - AS/A2 Philosophy of Religion and Religious Ethics for OCR, Nelson Thornes, 2004

- **COLE, P** - Access to Philosophy: Philosophy of Religion, Hodder & Stoughton, 2005

- **DEWAR, G** - Oxford Revision Guides: AS & A Level Religious Studies: Philosophy and Ethics Through Diagrams, Oxford University Press, 2009

- **JACKSON, R** - The God of Philosophy, The Philosophers' Magazine, 2001

- **JORDAN, A, LOCKYER, N, TATE, E** - Philosophy of Religion for A Level OCR Edition, Nelson Thornes, 2004

- **PHELAN, JW** - Philosophy Themes and Thinkers, Cambridge University Press, 2005

- **POXON, B** - Religious Studies AS Philosophy, PushMe press, 2012

- **EYRE, C, KNIGHT, R, ROWE, G** - OCR Religious Studies Philosophy and Ethics A2, Heinemann, 2009

- **TAYLOR, M** - OCR Philosophy of Religion for AS and A2, Routledge, 2009

- **WILKINSON, M & CAMPBELL, H** - Philosophy of Religion for A2 Level, Continuum, 2009

Lightning Source UK Ltd.
Milton Keynes UK
UKOW04f1526280314

229041UK00001B/1/P